25

ENGLISH·MAORI
MAORI·ENGLISH
DICTIONARY

ENGLISH·MAORI
MAORI·ENGLISH
DICTIONARY

BRUCE BIGGS

Library Resource Center
Renton Technical College
3000 N.E. 4th Street
Renton, WA 98056

AUCKLAND UNIVERSITY PRESS

I am grateful to the following for valuable comments and corrections: Margaret Mutu, Mary Penfold, Hillary Pound, Kare Leathem and Peter Ranby. While they are in no sense responsible for those that remain, many errors were eliminated by their careful reading of my manuscript.

499.442 BIGGS 1990

Biggs, Bruce, 1921-2000.

English-Maori, Maori-English
dictionary

First published 1990
Reprinted 1992, 1993, 1995, 1998, 2004, 2009
Auckland University Press
University of Auckland
Private Bag 92019, Auckland

ISBN 1 86940 056 9

© Bruce Briggs 1990

This book is copyright. Apart from any fair dealing for the purpose of private study, research, criticism, or review, as permitted under the Copyright Act, no part may be reproduced by any process without the prior permission of Auckland University Press.

Typeset by Typocrafters Ltd
Printed in China through Colorcraft Ltd, Hong Kong

CONTENTS

INTRODUCTION

While the four thousand or so entries in each section of this book leave it far from being a complete English–Maori and Maori–English dictionary, it has advantages over other available two-way dictionaries in that:

1. An attempt has been made in the English–Maori section to indicate the part of speech of Maori words according to an explicit, systematic classification that has proved to be relevant to the language.
2. Appropriate passive suffixes are indicated for passivable verbs (universals).
3. The quantity of all vowels is marked.
4. Maori words derived from English are included. Maori, like English, is a language that borrows words freely to express new concepts. The criterion for inclusion in this dictionary is simply whether or not a word is used by those competent in the language.
5. For grammatical particles a reference is given to relevant sections of the grammar book *Let's Learn Maori: a Guide to the Study of the Maori Language* (rev. ed., 1973) by Bruce Biggs (hereafter cited as LLM).

Spelling

Maori has ten consonant sounds, which are written as h, k, m, n, ng, p, r, t, w, wh.

Like other Polynesian languages, Maori has just five vowel sounds. They are represented conveniently by the five vowel letters of our English alphabet. Each vowel is either long or short. The distinction between long vowels and short vowels carries meaning and is all-pervasive (every vowel is either long or short).

There is an extraordinarily persistent misconception that it is only necessary to mark a long vowel in a word to distinguish it from some other word which differs only by having a short vowel (e.g., *papa, papaa*). Nothing could be further from the truth. As every Maori vowel is either long or short, it is necessary to indicate the quantity of each and every one. In this dictionary long vowels are written as double vowels. Single vowels are short.

Most early and some contemporary Maori text does not distinguish between long and short vowels. Some recent texts distinguish long vowels by a macron or short bar placed over the vowel. Either convention should occasion no difficulty to users of this dictionary because of the alphabetic order adopted, which keeps Maori words differing only by vowel length in adjacent positions (see the section on Maori–English below).

Hyphens are used in two ways in the dictionary:

1. Before or after a space to indicate an affix (e.g., *kite-a*). This has no phonetic significance.
2. To join two words considered to be a sense unit (e.g., *mata-uu* (nipple)). In such cases the hyphen indicates that the components of the compound are pronounced as separate words.

Parentheses within Maori words indicate that the parenthesised letter or letters may be omitted without substantially altering the meaning of the word, e.g., *ra(ra)ta, paakaru(karu), ho(o)u, (w)hea*.

Pronunciation

It is not possible to define pronunciation precisely by the written word, but comparison with English words will be helpful to those unfamiliar with Maori. As the language is spelt phonemically it is only necessary to indicate the pronunciation of each consonant and vowel, and each vowel combination (diphthong). The comparisons are with New Zealand English. For a more detailed discussion of Maori pronunciation see LLM, 54.

Consonants

Pronounce *h, k, m, n, p, r, t, w* approximately as in English.

Pronounce *ng* as in 'singer' (not as in 'finger') and *wh* as f or as wh in 'whale'.

Vowels

Pronounce short *a* as in 'mutt', long *aa* as in Haas: *mata* (raw), *Maata* (Martha), *mataa* (flint, bullet).

Pronounce *e* as in 'merry, ferry', *ee* as in 'Mary, fairy': *keke* (cake), *kekee* (creak), *keekee* (armpit).

Pronounce *i* as in 'pip', *ii* as in 'peep': *pipi* (cockle), *piipii* (chick), *pipii* (ooze out).

Pronounce *o* as in 'port', *oo* as in 'porn': *poti* (boat), *pooti* (vote), *koko* (corner), *kookoo* (parson bird or tui).

Pronounce *u* as in 'put', *uu* as *oo* in 'pool': *kuku* (mussel), *kuukuu* (pigeon), *puru* (plug), *puuru* (bull).

Diphthongs

Pronounce *ae* and *aae* as in 'sigh', *ai* and *aai* as in 'sighing': *pae* (perch), *aae* (yes), *kainga* (eaten), *kaainga* (home).

Pronounce *ao* and *aao* as in 'cow' (New Zealand pronunciation) and *au* and *aau* as in 'cow' (Canadian pronunciation), and *ou* and *oou* as in 'low': *tao* (cook), *kaao* (no), *tau* (settle, perch), *taau* (your), *tou* (backside, bum), *toou* (your).

Pronounce *ei* as in 'hay' and *ie* as in Russian 'nyet': *kei* (at), *kiekie* (a plant used in weaving).

Pronounce *eo* and *eu* as in 'jello' and 'Nehru', leaving out the consonants: *reo* (language), *heu* (shave).

Rhyme *ea* with 'hair', *ia* with 'hear', *oa* with 'oar' and *ua* with 'sewer': *whea?* (where?), *whia?* (how many), *hoa* (friend), *hua* (fruit).

Pronounce *oi* as in 'boy' and *oe* as in 'or wet' leaving off the t: *koi* (sharp), *koe* (you).

Rhyme *iu* with 'few' and *io* with 'Rio': *whiu* (whip, punish), *whio* (whistle).

Stress

Apply stress (accent) to words containing less than six vowels according to the following ordered rules. (Words containing more than six vowels are stressed as two words even if written as one.)

1. Stress the first long vowel, if there is one: MAArama, wheTUU, HAAngii, KOOhanga, wikiTOOria.
2. Stress a non-final diphthong if there is one: WAItangi, MAAOritanga, paRAAIhe, kaRAUna, AOtea, kapoREIhana.
3. If there is no double vowel and no non-final diphthong stress the first vowel in the word: WAhine, RAngatira, MArama, KAhawai.

For a more detailed account of stress placement see LLM, 54.4, 54.5.

Dictionary entries

English–Maori entries

The order of the English–Maori section follows the English alphabet. Each entry consists of an English word or phrase followed by a colon (:) and a Maori equivalent. Where there are several Maori words equivalent to the English headword, which is usually the case, each one is separated by a comma. In many cases the part of speech of the Maori word is indicated either by an appropriate passive ending (or parenthesised passive form) indicating a Universal, or by *N, A, P, L* or *Pnl.* indicating Noun, Stative-adjective, Participle, Locative, Personal respectively. Universals may be used nominally, and as active and passive verbs; Stative-adjectives may be used as nouns and as verbs, but do not take passive terminations; Participles are a subclass of Stative-adjectives which may not be used as nouns. Locatives are never used verbally and do not normally take an article; Personals take the Proper Article. See LLM Section 16 for a more detailed explanation of the parts of speech of Maori.

Maori–English entries

In the Maori to English section of the dictionary each entry consists of a headword, which ends with a colon (:), and a gloss, which ends with a period (.). As mentioned above, parentheses within a headword indicate that the parenthesised letters may be pronounced or not, without substantially altering the meaning of the word.

Where a headword, in at least one of its meanings, may take a passive suffix, an appropriate form of the suffix is indicated (e.g., *inu -mia*). If the base itself is altered in the passive, the entire passive form is given in parentheses (e.g., *tiki, (tiikina)*).

Headwords are arranged in the following alphabetical order: *aa, a, ee, e, h, ii, i, k, m, n, ng, oo, o, p, r, t, uu, u, w, wh.*

Notice particularly that the digraphs *ng* and *wh* are treated as single letters following *n* and *w* respectively. Note also that words like *paapaa, papaa, papa*, which differ only by the quantity of their vowels, and words that differ only by a hyphen (*-tia, tia*) will be kept together. Parentheses are ignored, so pairs such as *ii, i(i)* and *kaa, ka(a)* will also be found next to each other.

In many Maori words, but not all, the letter *h* may sometimes appear as *wh* because of dialect differences. The word *hea?*

(where?) is often spoken and written *whea?*, for example. In this dictionary many such words are written with a parenthesised *(w)* so this word is written *(w)hea* and found under WH. If you are checking for the meaning of a word beginning with *h* and cannot find it under H, look also under WH.

The English glosses for each Maori headword often consist of a number of English words separated by commas and/or semicolons. The words between semicolons are considered to be related in meaning. Those separated by a semicolon differ in meaning and may indicate that a homonym is involved. Study the following entry and you will see that there are two sets of meanings separated by a semicolon: *mata*: eye, face, countenance; green, unripe, raw, uncooked.

The short Maori words called particles usually lack lexical meaning and can best be understood by reference to a grammar. Where appropriate, references are provided to relevant section(s) in LLM. (For example, *ana*: cave, cavern; *postposed verbal particle* (LLM 36.); his, her (LLM 14.1–2); when (LLM 8.1, 53.3).

The causative prefix *whaka-* regularly derives transitive verbs from intransitive verbs. So *mate* (die), *whakamate* (kill); *tupu* (grow), *whakatupu* (rear, raise (as plants etc.)). Causative transitive verbs are formed from transitive verbs by prefixing *whaka-*. So *inu* (drink), *whakainu* (cause to drink, give drink); *rongo* (hear), *whakarongo* (listen). In this dictionary many words beginning with *whaka-*, especially those whose meanings are not obviously derived from the meaning of the base, are listed alphabetically under WH. If, however, an entry is not found there, look for the base entry and deduce an appropriate causative meaning. For example, *whakamahi* does not warrant a separate entry because its meaning (cause to work, set to work) is predictable from *mahi* (work) plus the meaning of *whaka-*.

Library Resource Center
Renton Technical College
3000 N.E. 4th Street
Renton, WA 98056

11

Abbreviations

a.	adjective.
A	stative adjective class base.
ad.	adverb.
L	locative class base.
n.	noun.
N	noun class base.
P	participle class base.
part.	participle.
pl.	plural.
Pnl.	personal class base.
pron.	pronoun.
v.	verb.
v.i.	intransitive verb.
v.t.	transitive verb.

ENGLISH–MAORI

A

a, an: he, teetahi (LLM, 2.1).
abandon: whakarere
  (whakareerea).
abashed: whakamaa.
abate: maahaki *P*, maarie *P*, iti
  haere.
abbreviate: whakapoto-a.
abdomen: puku *N*, koopuu *N*,
  kona *N*, takapuu *N*.
abduct: ka(w)haki-na.
abhor: whakakino-tia.
abide: noho-ia.
ability: kaha *A*, rawe.
able: aahei, kaha *A*.
abode: kaainga *N*.
abolish: whakakore-tia,
  whakakaahore-tia, peehi-a.
abominable: whakarihariha,
  weriweri, wetiweti.
aboriginal (indigenous):
  maaori.
aborigine: tangata whenua.
abortion: mate-roto,
  whakatahe *N*.
abound: hua, nui, tini *A*.
about (approximately): tata ki.
about (concerning): e paa ana
  ki, mo (LLM, 18.32).
above: kei/i runga.
abridge: whakapoto-a.
abscess: puku, taapoa.
absent: ngaro.
absorbed: mimiti *A*.
abundance, abundant: nui *A*.
abuse, abusive: kanga-a,
  whaka-kino-tia.
accede: whakaae-tia.

accelerate: whakahohori-tia.
accept: tango-hia, whakaaetia.
accident: mea tuupono, aituaa.
accommodation: nohoanga,
  whare noho.
accompany: haere tahi.
accomplice: hoa *N*.
accomplish, accomplished: tae
  (taaea), oti *P*.
accordingly: heoi, na/no reira.
account (bill): kaute *N*, pire *N*.
accurate: tika *A*, tootika *A*.
accuse: whakapae-a.
accustomed: taunga-tia, waia
  P.
ache: mamae *A*.
ache (head): aanini.
achieve: tae (taaea) (ki).
acid (taste): kawa *A*.
acknowledge (authority):
  whakamana-a.
acknowledge (agree with):
  whakaae-tia.
acquire: whiwhi *A*.
acquired, be: riro *P*.
acre: eka *N*.
across: ki taawaahi.
across, lie: takoto koopae.
action: mahi-a.
action-song: waiata-a-ringa.
add (on, to): apiti-ria, hono-a,
  huihui-a.
address *v*.: koorero-tia,
  whaikoorero.
address *n*.: kaainga (noho) *N*.
adept: maatau-ria, moohio-tia,
  rawe *A*.

adhere: piri *A*, rapa-ngia (ki).

adjourn (a meeting): hiki-tia, nuku-hia.

adjust: whakarite-a.

admirable: rangatira *A*.

admiral: aatamira *N*.

admire: mihi-a, miiharo-tia.

admit (let in): tuku-a kia tomo.

admit (own up): whaaki-na.

adopt (a child): whaangai-a.

adopted child: tamaiti atawhai, tamaiti whaangai, taurima.

adorn: whakapaipai-tia, raakei-tia.

adrift: maanu *P*, tere *A*.

adult: kaumaatua-tia, pakeke *A*.

adulterate: whakananu-a, whakaranu.

adultery: puuremu-tia.

advantage: pai *A*, huhuatanga *N*.

adversity: mate *A*, hee *A*.

advertise: paanui-tia.

advertisement: paanui.

advertising: paanuitanga.

adze: kapu, waru.

aeroplane: waka-rererangi, wakarere.

affect: paa-ngia.

affection: aroha-tia, aroha-ina.

affirm: whakawhiu-a, whakamamae-tia.

affray: whawhai-tia.

afloat: maanu *P*, rewa.

afraid: mataku *A*, paawera *A*, wehi *A*.

after: muri *L*.

afterbirth: whenua *N*, ewe *N*.

afternoon: ahiahi *A*, te heketanga o te raa.

afterwards: i muri.

again: anoo.

age: pakeke.

agenda: raarangi take.

agent: maangai *N*.

agitate: ueue.

agree: whakaae-tia (ki).

agreed, be: rite *P*.

agreeable: aahuareka, puurotu, pai *A*.

agreement (legal): kirimini *N*.

agriculture: ahu-whenua.

ahead: i mua, whakamua.

aim (at target): whakakeko.

aim (goal): whaainga *N*.

alarmed: mataku *A*, ohorere.

alas: auee-tia.

albatross: toroa *N*.

alike: rite *A*.

alive: ora *A*.

all: katoa *N*.

allayed: maariri *P*.

allow: tuku-a.

alloy: meetara whakaranu *N*.

almost: waahi iti, tata, tata noa ki.

alone: anake.

aloof, be: tuu kee.

alphabet: raarangi reta.

alphabetise: whakaraarangi reta.

also: hoki *particle* (LLM,47).

altar: aata *N*.

alter: whakaahua kee, whakaputa kee.

altered: rere kee.

alternate: whakawhitiwhiti.

although: ahakoa.

always: i ngaa waa katoa.

am: *See under* **be**.

ambassador: maangai (o te kaawanatanga).

amble (of horse): aamara.

ambulance: waka tuuroro.

ambush: haupapa-tia, pehipehia, rau-a.

amend: whakatikatika-ina.

amendment (legal): menemana *N.*

amidst: i waenganui.

ammunition: haamanu *N*, mataa *N*, kariri *N.*

among: i waenganui, i roto.

amuse: whakataakaro-tia, whakarawe-a.

anaesthesia: whakakore mamae.

anaesthetic: rongoa whakakore mamae.

anaesthetist: taakuta whakakore mamae.

anal sphincter: takini o te tou.

analyse: taatari-tia.

ancestor: tupuna *N*, tipuna *N* (*pl.* tuupuna, tiipuna).

ancestry: kaawai *N.*

anchor: punga-a, haika *N.*

anchorage: tauranga *N*, urunga *N.*

angel: anahera *N.*

angle: tuke, koki, whatianga *N.*

Anglican: Mihingare.

angry: pukuriri, riri-a.

animal: kararehe *N.*

ankle: pona.

annihilate: whakangaro-mia, whakakore-tia.

annoy: whakatoi, whakatenetene.

annoyed: whanowhanoaa, kaarangirangi, rikarika.

annul: whakakaahore-tia, whakakore-tia.

anoint: whakawahi-a.

anorexia: mate hiakai-kore.

another: teetahi atu.

answer: whakahoki-a (ki), whakautu-a.

ant: poopokorua *N*, pokorua *N*, pokopokorua *N.*

antagonist: hoa-whawhai *N.*

anus: puta (o te tou), whero.

anxious, anxiety: aawangawanga, maaharahara-tia.

apostle: aapotoro *N.*

appeal (ask, beg): inoi-a.

appeal (legal): piira *N.*

appear: puta *A.*

appearance *n.*: aahua *N.*

appease: whakamaarie-tia.

appeased, be: maarie *P*, mauru *P.*

appetite: hiakai, matekai.

apple: aaporo *N.*

appliance (household): taputapu *N.*

applicant: kai-tono.

application (e.g., job): tono.

apply: tono-a.

appoint: whakarite-a, tohu-a.

apprehensive: maanukanuka *A*, paawera *A*, manawapaa, ohooho.

approach: whakatata-ngia.

appropriate *a.*: tika *A.*

appropriate *v.*: tango-hia, taapui-a.

approve: whakapai-a, whakaaetia.

approved: pai-ngia.
April: Aaperira *Pnl.*
apron: maro *N*, pini *N*.
are: *See under* **be.**
argue: totohe (toohea).
arise: ara, maranga, whakatika.
arithmetic: whika *N*.
arm: ringa(ringa).
armpit: keekee *N*.
army: ope *N*, taua *N*.
aromatic: kakara.
arouse: whakaara-hia,
   whakaoho-kia.
arrange: whakarite-a,
   whakataakotokoto-ria.
arrive: tae (taaea), uu-ngia (ki),
   tau, eke, tatuu.
arrogant: whakakake-a,
   whakahiihii.
arrow: pere-a.
artery: uaua.
articulate (pronounce):
   whakahua-tia.
artist: tohunga *N*.
ascend: kake-a, piki-tia.
ascent: pikitanga *N*.
ashamed: whakamaa.
ashes: pungarehu *N*.
ashore: ki uta.
aside: ki tahaki.
ask (question): ui-a (ki), paatai-
   ngia (ki).
ask for (favour): inoi-a, tono-a,
   kii-a.
asleep: moe-a.
aspect: anganga *N*.
ass: kaaihe *N*.
assault: whakaeke-a.
assemblage: huihuinga tangata,
   whakaminenga *N*.

assemble: whakamine-a, hui-a.
assembled, be: emi *P*, ruupeke
   P.
assent: whakaae-tia.
assert: koorero-tia.
assess: taatari-tia.
assessor (legal): ateha *N*.
asset: rawa *N*.
assiduous: mamahi, pukumahi.
assist: aawhina-tia.
assistant: kai-aawhina.
associate with: whakahoa,
   whakapaa.
asterisk: whetuu.
asthma: huango, kume.
atoned for, be: ea *P*.
attack: huaki-na.
attain: tae (taaea).
attempt: whakamaatau-ria.
attend: whakarongo-hia (ki).
auction: maakete *N*.
auctioneer: kaimaakete.
audit (accounts): taatari
   (kaute).
audit (listen to): whakarongo-
   hia (ki).
auditor (of accounts): otita *N*.
auger: wiri.
August: Akuhata *Pnl.*
aunt: whaaea (keekee), matua
   (keekee).
Australia: Ahitereiria.
authority: mana, tikanga *N*.
autumn: ngahuru *N*.
available: waatea *A*.
available, make:
   whakawaatea-hia.
avaricious: apo, kaiponu.
avenge: rapu utu, ngaki
   mate.

avenged: ea *P.*
avert: kaupare-a.
awake: ara *A*, oho *A*.
awaken: whakaara-hia,
  whakaoho-kia.

award *v.*: whakawhiwhi-a,
  tuku-a.
award *n.*: paraaihe, tohu.
awry: parori.
axe: toki *N*.

B

baby: peepi *N*, nepa *N*.
bachelor: taitama, taahae.
back (rear): muri *L*.
back (of body): tuaraa *N*.
backbone: iwi tuaraa.
backed (of sails): puuawhe-a.
backside: kootore *N*.
backstay: tuku-roa.
backwards: whakamuri-a.
backwater: muriwai.
bacon: peekana *N*.
bad (evil): kino *A*.
bad (rotten): piro *A*, pirau *A*.
baffled: rehe-a.
bag: peeke *N*, puutea *N*,
  whakarino.
bail (liquids): ehu-a, taa-ngia.
bailer: tataa, tiiheru.
bait: moounu-tia, maaunu-tia,
  (poa)poa.
bake: tunu-a.
balance (remainder): toenga *N*.
balance (accounts):
  whakataurite-a (kaute).
bald: paakira *A*.
balked: rehe-a.
ball: paoro *N*, pooro *N*, poi-a,
  pookai-tia.
band (headband): pare.

band (girdle, bond): ruruku-tia.
band (musical): peene *N*,
  roopuu whakatangitangi.
band (of people): apa *N*, ohu
  N, ope *N*.
bandage: takai-a.
banish: pei-a, pana-a.
bank (financial): peeke *N*.
bank (earth): taha *A*, tahataha
  N, pare-nga *N*, tuuparipari
  N.
bank (shallow): taahuna *N*,
  ranga.
bar (of harbour, river): taahuna
  N.
barb: kaaniwha *N*,
  whakakaaniwha.
barbarian, barbarous: mohoao
  N.
bare: maarakerake *A*,
  maamore, moremore.
bare (unclothed): kirikau,
  hahake.
bargeboard: maihi *N*.
bark *v.*: tau, au, pahu(pahu).
bark *n.*: kiri raakau, hiako,
  peha.
barkless: ngorengore.
barley: paare(i) *N*.

barnacle: koromaaungaunga *N*.
barracouta: mangaa *N*.
barrel: kaaho *N*.
barren (of woman): puku-paa, pakoro *A*.
barren (of land): tiitoohea *A*.
barricade: aarai-a, tauaarai-tia, paa-ia.
barter: hoko-na, hokohoko.
basalt: karaa *N*.
base *n*.: puutake.
basin: peihana *N*.
bask (in sun): inaina, paainaina.
basket (generic): kete *N*.
basket (small, for cooked food): kono *N*, rourou *N*, paaroo *N*.
bastard: pooriro *N*, poorori *N*, tiiraumoko *N*.
bat (creature): pekapeka *N*.
bathe: kaukau, horoi-a.
batten: kaahoo *N*, paatene *N*.
battery: paatiri *N*.
battle: parekura *N*, pakanga.
bawl: haamama, pararee, ngangaa.
bay: kokoru *N*.
bayonet: peeneti *N*.
be: Maori has no direct equivalent of the verb to be. See section on nominal sentences in LLM.
beach: one *N*.
beak: ngutu manu, timo.
beam: kurupae *N*.
bean: piini *N*.
bear *v*.: kawe-a, amo-hia, hari-a, mau-ria.
bear (child): whakawhaanau-tia.

bear (fruit): hua.
bear (pain): manawa nui.
beard: paahau *N*, paihau *N*.
bearer: kaiamo *N*, kaimau *N*.
beast: kararehe *N*.
beat: tuki-a, kuru-a, patu-a, taa-ia.
beat (of heart): patupatu, panapana, kapakapa.
beat (one another): taupatupatu.
beaten, defeated: piiti *A*, mate *A*, hinga *P*, raru *A*.
beater: paoi, tuki.
beautiful: aataahua *A*, huumarie *N*.
because: na/no/mo/ta te mea.
beckon: taawhiri-tia, poowhiri-tia.
bed: moenga *N*.
be-dewed: haumaakuu *A*.
bedroom: whare moe, waahi moe.
bee: pii *N*.
beech: tawai *N*.
beef: miiti kau *N*, piiwhi *N*.
beer: pia *N*.
befall: pono, tuupono.
before: no/kei/ki/i mua.
beg: inoi-a, pati.
beget: ai-tia.
begin: tiimata-ria.
beginning: tiimatanga *N*.
beguile: whakaware-a, (whaka)patipati, whakawai-a.
behind: kei/ki/i/hei muri.
behind (a solid object): kei/ki/i/hei tua.

behold: interjection: na!, nana!, anaa!, kaaore!, (poet.).

behold *v.*: titiro, tirohia.

belch: kuupaa, puupaa, tokopuhake.

belief, believe: whakapono-ngia.

belittle: whakahaawea-tia.

bell: pere *N*.

bellbird: korimako *N*, koopara *N*.

bellows: pouahi.

belly: koopuu *N*, puku *A*, manawa *N*.

below: kei/ki/i/hei raro.

belt: whiitiki-ria, taatua.

bend, bent: piko *A*, whakapiko-a, koowhana, noni.

bend (of arm or leg): huupeke-tia.

bend (of knees): turi peepeke.

benzine: penehini *N*.

berry: kaakano *N*.

beseech: inoi-a.

beset: awhi-tia, mui-a.

beside: kei/ki/i/hei te taha.

beside (oneself): poorangi, wairangi.

besides: haaunga.

besiege: whakapae-a.

besmear: pani-a.

bespeak: taunaha-tia, tapatapa-ia.

best: pai rawa, tino pai.

bestir oneself: korikori.

betrayal: kaikai wai-uu.

betroth: taumau-tia, whakaihi-a.

better, it is: engari, pai atu.

between: kei/ki/hei/i waenganui.

bevel: peewara.

bewildered: pooauau *A*, hiirawerawe.

bewitch: maakutu-ria.

beyond: ki/i/kei/hei koo atu.

beyond (a solid object): ki/i/kei/hei tua atu.

Bible: paipera *N*.

bier: amo-hia, kauhoa, atamira *N*.

big: nui *A*, rahi *A*.

bight (bay): kokorutanga *N*.

bilge: riu *N*.

bilingual: reo-rua.

bill (account): kaute.

bill (beak): ngutu manu, timo.

bill (political): pire *N*.

billiards: piriota.

bind: here-a, hohou-tia, takai-a.

bindweed: poohue *N*.

bird: manu *N*.

birth: whaanautanga *N*.

biscuit: piihikete *N*.

bishop: piihopa *N*.

bit: waahi, maramara *N*.

bit (for horse): pita.

bit (of drill): niho.

bite: ngau-a.

bite (of fish at line): kakai.

bitter: kawa *A*.

bittern: huurepo *N*, matuku *N*.

black: mangu *A*, pango *A*.

Black: Mangumangu.

blacksmith: parakimete *N*.

bladder: toongaa-mimi *N*.

blade: rau *N*.

blame: hee *A*, whakahee-ngia.
blanket: paraikete *N*.
blaze: toro, mura.
bleed: toto.
bless: whakapai-ngia.
blighted: koomae.
blind *a.*: matapoo, kaapoo, pohe.
blind *n.*: paraina.
blink: kimo.
blistered: taangorongoro, kopuu, kooipuipu.
block (of land): poraka.
block (of wood): poro.
blocked up: (puru)puru-a, aarai-tia, kati-a, paa-ia, puni *A*.
blockhead: moho.
blood: toto *A*.
blood pressure: te kaha o te ia toto.
bloody: puutoto.
blossom: pua, puaawai.
blow *v.*: pupuhi (puuhia).
blow *n.*: kuru-a, moto-kia.
blue: puruu.
blunt: puhuki, punuki.
bluster: whakatuupehupehu.
boar: taariana, tame poaka.
board (plank): papa.
board (committee): poari.
boast: whakaputa, whakakake, whakatuu, paakiwaha.
boat: poti *N*, waka *N*.
body: tinana *N*.
bog: repo *N*.
boggy: oru, ooruru, taapokopoko.
boil *v.*: koropupuu, huu, paaera-tia.

boil *n.*: wheewhee *N*.
boisterous: tuuperepere.
bold: toa *A*, maaia *A*.
bolt *v.*: whakarawa-tia.
bolt (of a horse): kahaki-na.
bone: iwi *N*, wheua *N*.
book: pukapuka *N*.
boot: puutu *N*.
booth: wharau.
booty: paarurenga, parakete.
border (of garment): remu *N*.
border (of land): rohe-a.
bore *v.*: wiri, ore-a, poka-ina.
bored: hoohaa *A*.
born: whaanau *A*.
bosom: uma *N*, poho *N*.
boss (one in charge): paahi, po(o)hi, rangatira.
both: e rua, e rua; toona rua, ngaatahi.
bottle: paatara *N*, pounamu *N*, ipu *N*.
bottom: raro *L*.
bough: peka *A*, manga *N*.
boundary: rohe-a, raina *N*.
bow *v.*: tuuohu, koropiko.
bow *n.*: ihu *N*.
bow (weapon, shape): koopere *N*.
bowels: wheekau *N*, ngaakau *N*.
bowl: kumete *N*, oko *N*.
box *v.*: (mo)moto-kia, me(ke)meke-hia.
box *n.*: pouaka *N*.
boy: poai *N*, taitama *N*, tamaiti *N*.
brace: tauteka, hookai.
brackish: maataitai.
brains: roro *N*.

brake: pereki *N*.
bramble: taataraamoa *N*.
bran: paapapa.
branch: manga *N*, peka-ina.
branchless: morimori.
brand: parani-tia.
brandish: (rure)rure-a, piioi-tia,
poipoi-a.
brass: paraahi.
brave: maaia *A*, toa *A*.
bread: paraaoa *N*, roohi *N*.
break in pieces: tataa-ngia.
breakfast: parakuihi.
breast: uma *N*, poho *N*, uu *N*.
breastwork: parepare.
breath: manawa *N*, haa *N*.
breath (take breath):
whakangaa, whakataa i te
manawa, whakaea.
breathe: whakaeaea.
breed (kind): momo.
breeze: hau, muri, hauora.
brick: pereki *N*.
bridge: piriti *N*, arawhata
N.
bridle: paraire *N*.
brig: pereki *N*.
bright: piiata *A*, kanapa.
brim: ngutu *N*, paarua.
brimful: puurena.
brimstone: ngaawhaariki.
bring: mau(-ria) mai, hari(-a)
mai.
brink: tahataha.
bristle: huruhuru.
bristling: taatarahake.
broach, to: rara.
broad: whaanui *A*.
broadcast (radio): paaho.
broadcast (as seed): rui-a.

broadside on: rara, koopae,
koronae.
broil: tunu-a.
broken: pakaru *A*, whati-ia,
poro-a.
brook: manga *N*, wai *N*.
broom: puruuma *N*.
brother (girl speaking):
tungaane *N*.
brother (older boy speaking):
teina *N* (*pl.* teeina).
**brother (younger boy
speaking):** tuakana *N* (*pl.*
tuaakana).
brother-in-law: taokete *N*.
brow (forehead): rae *N*.
brown: paakaakaa, paraaone.
bruised: kooparu *A*, maruu *P*.
brush: paraihe *N*.
brushwood: heuheu *N*, puaka
N.
bubble *v.*: puu, pupuu,
koropupuu.
bucket: peere *N*, paakete *N*.
bugle: piukera, piukara.
build: hanga-a.
bull: pu(u)ru *N*.
bullock: ookiha *N*.
bulrush: raupoo *N*.
bunch: puutoi, herehere.
**bunched together (of people
moving):** koopuni *A*.
bunched up (as hair): puhipuhi.
bundle: paihere-tia.
bung: puru-a.
buoy: kaarewa.
burden: kawenga *N*, wahanga
N, piikau.
burial place: urupaa *N*, waahi
tapu.

burn: kaa, ngiha.
burnt: wera *A*.
burr: piripiri *N*.
burrow: rua *N*.
burst: pahuu, papaa, ngawhaa.
bus: pahi *N*.
bush (forest): ngahere *N*, puihi
   N, ngaaherehere *N*.
bush lawyer (plant):
   taataraamoa *N*.
bushel: puuhera *N*.
business (occupation): mahi.
busy: raru(raru).
but: engari, erangi, otiraa.
but rather: engari, erangi.
butcher: putia *N*, puha *N*.

butcher-knife: oka, puha *N*.
butt *v.*: tuki-a.
butt, *n.*: poro.
butter: pata *N*.
butterfly: (pee)pepe *N*.
buttocks: papa *N*.
button: paatene *N*.
buy: hoko-na.
buyer: kaihoko *N*.
buzz: wheo(wheo).
by (agentive): na, e (LLM, 7.1).
by (near to): i (LLM, 11.3), kei
   (11.2).
by means of: ki, na.
by way of: ma (LLM, 18.33),
   na.

C

cabbage: kaapeti *N*.
cabbage-tree: tii-koouka, tii-
   kaauka.
cake: keke *N*.
calabash: ipu *N*, tahaa *N*,
   kiiaka *N*.
calamity: aituaa *A*.
calculate: tatau (tauria).
calendar: maramataka.
calf: kaawhe.
calico: kareko.
California: Karapoonia.
calk: mono-kia.
call: karanga-tia.
call (a dog): moimoi.
call (name): hua-ina, tapa-ia.
calloused: uutonga-tia.
calm: marino *A*, aaio *A*.

camel: kaamera *N*.
camera: kaamera *N*.
can: tini *N*.
can-opener: tiiwara tini.
Canada: Kaanata *L*.
cancer: mate pukupuku.
candle: kaanara *N*.
cannabis: kanapihi *N*.
cannon: puu repo.
canoe: waka *N*.
cap: pootae-a.
capable: maaia *A*, kakama.
captain: kaapene *N*.
captive *n.*: herehere.
captive *part.*: mau herehere.
capture: whakahere-a.
captured: mau herehere.
car: motokaa *N*, motukaa *N*.

card: kaari *N.*
cardiac arrest: manawa tuu.
careful: tuupato.
careless: whakaaro-kore,
koretake.
cargo: utanga.
carpenter: kaamura *N.*
carpentry: mahi kaamura.
carpet: whaariki-tia, takapau
N, kaapeti *N.*
carried away: rere *A*, riro *P.*
carrier: kai amo *N*, kai mau.
carrot: kaareti.
carry: kawe-a, hari-a, mau-ria.
carry (in the arms): hiki-tia,
tapuhi-tia.
carry (off by force):
ka(w)haki-na.
carry (on a litter): amo-hia,
kauhoa.
carry (on a pole): tauteka.
carry (on the back): piikau-tia,
waha-a.
carry (on the shoulder):
amo-hia.
cart: kaata *N.*
cartridge: kariri *N.*
cartridge-belt: haamanu *N*,
whiitiki kariri.
carve: whakairo-hia.
carved figure: tekoteko *N*, tiki
N.
case: keehi *N.*
case, in that: mehemea i
peenaa, mehemea koia
teenaa.
case, in either: mehemea i
peenei i peeraa raanei.
cask: kaaho *N.*
cast (off): whakarere-a.

cast (on shore): pae-a.
cast (throw): maka-a, panga-a,
whiu-a.
cat: ngeru *N*, tori *N*, poti *N.*
catalogue: raarangi-tia.
cataract (waterfall): rere,
taaheke.
catch: hopu-kia, tango-hia.
catch (at): kapo-hia.
catch (in a net): hao-a.
catechise: paatai-a, (ui)uia.
catechism: katikiihama *N.*
caterpillar: anuhe *N.*
cat's cradle: whai.
caul: (kahu)kahu.
cauliflower: kareparaoa.
cause *v.*: mea-tia, meinga.
cause *n.*: take, puutake.
caution, cautious: tuupato *A*,
whakatuupato-ria.
cave: ana *N.*
cease: mutu *P*, kaati!
cement: raima.
cemetery: urupaa *N*, toma *N*,
waahi tapu.
centipede: weri *N.*
centre: waenganui *L.*
certain (be sure): moohio
tuuturu, tino moohio.
certain (particular): teetahi, (*pl.*
eetahi).
certificate: tiwhikete *N.*
chaff: paapapa.
chain: tiini *N*, mekameka *N.*
chair: tuuru *N.*
chairman/person: tiamana *N*,
heamana *N*, teepu *N.*
chalk: tioka *N.*
challenge: taki-na.
champ: katikati.

change: whakarere kee, kawe kee, whakaputa kee.
change (of wind): koorure.
channel: awa *N*.
chant: waiata-tia, karakia-tia, paatere *A*.
chaplet: tuupare.
chapped: raupaa, ngaatata, taapaa.
chapter: upoko *N*.
char: huhunu (hunuhunua).
character: aahua *N*.
charcoal: waro *N*.
charge: huaki.
charge (debit): utu-a.
chariot: hariata *N*.
charm: karakia-tia.
chart: mapi *N*.
chase: (aru)aru-mia, (whai)whai-a.
chasm: ngaatata *A*, rua.
chastise: whiu-a.
chatter: koorerorero.
cheek: paapaaringa *N*.
cheek (give): whakatoi-tia.
cheerful: manahau, ngahau.
cheese: tiihi *N*.
chemist: keemihi *N*.
cheque: haki *N*.
cherish: whakatapu-ria, whakaahuru-tia, tohu-ngia, tiaki-na.
chest: poho, uma.
chew: ngaungau-a.
chicken: pii *N*.
chickweed: kohukohu.
chief: rangatira *A*, ariki.
chilblain: maangiongio.
child: tamaiti *N*, koohungahunga *N*.

childhood: tamarikitanga *N*.
children: tamariki *A*.
chimney: tuumere *N*, tiimera *N*.
chin: kau(w)ae *N*.
China: Tiaina.
Chinese: Hainamana.
chink: riwha.
chip *v.*: (ha)hau-a, tarai-a.
chip *n.*: maramara *N*.
chipped: riwha, hawa.
chirp: pekii.
chisel: whao-a, purupuru.
chocolate: tiakerete *N*, hokorete *N*.
choice: mea whiriwhiri, mea tohu.
choir: koaea *N*.
choke: nanati (naatia).
choked: raaoa *A*.
choose: whiriwhiri-a, tohungia.
chop: tapahi-a, tarai-a.
chop (off): momotu (motuhia), poouto-kia.
Christ: (Te) Karaiti *Pnl*.
Christmas: Kirihimete *N*.
Christmas tree: pohutukawa *N*.
chrysalis: tuungoungou.
church: haahi *N*, whare karakia.
churlish: houkeke.
cicada: kihikihi, taatarakihi.
circle *n.*: porowhita.
circuitous: aawhio.
circumference: pae.
circumstance: aahuatanga *N*.
citizen: tangata whenua.
citizenship: tangata-whenuatanga.
clamp *n.*: kuku.

clandestine: puku.
clap: pakipaki.
clatter: tatangi.
claw: matikuku *N*, maikuku *N*, (ra)rapi-hia.
clay: uku.
clean: maa *A*.
cleanse: horoi-a.
clear *a*.: aatea *A*, maarama *A*.
clear *v*.: tahi-a, heuheu-tia, waere-a.
clearing (in bush): waerenga *N*.
cleave: (waa)waahi-a, tiiwara-hia.
cleft *n*.: riwha, paakohu.
clergy: minita, nga.
clerk: karaka *N*.
clever: muurere, kakama *A*.
cliff: pari *A*.
climb: kake-a, piki-tia.
cling (adhere): piri.
cling on to something: (pu)puri-tia.
cloak: (kaa)kahu-ria.
clock: karaka *N*.
clod: kerepei, paioneone.
close (near): tata *A*, paatata *A*.
close *v*.: tuutaki-na, kopi-a, kuku-a, kati-a, kapi-a.
close (a legal case): kopi-a.
close (eyes): (ne)newha, kapi-a.
closely woven: mangungu.
clot *n*.: tepe.
clot (of blood): puku toto.
clot (congeal): tetepe, tepetepe.
clothe: kaakahu-ria, kuhu kaakahu.
clothes: kaakahu, kaka *N*, puuweru *N*.
cloud: kapua *N*, ao-hia.

cloudy: koonguu, taamaru-tia.
club *v*., *n*.: patu-a, wahaika *N*, mere *N*, kotiate *N*.
clubfooted: hape.
clump: motu.
clumsy: pakihawa, tupehau.
cluster: mui-a, poohuuhuu, raapoi-tia, tautau.
clutch: aurara, rarapa.
coal: waro.
coast: tahatika *N*, takutai *N*, aakau *N*, tahatai *N*, taatahi *L*, tai *L*.
coat: koti *N*.
coax: pati, whakapati(pati).
cobweb: tukutuku, whare puungaawere(were).
cock (bird): piikaokao *N*.
cock (penis): ure *N*.
cockle: huangi *N*, huu(w)ai *N*, tuangi *N*, pipi.
coffee: kawhe *N*.
coffin: kaawhena.
cohabit: noho-ia, moe-a, ai-tia.
coil: whakakoro-meke, koru, pookai-a.
cold *a*.: makariri *A*, maatao *A*, koopeke *A*.
cold (virus infection): taruwhiti, taiawa, rewharewha, mate maremare.
collarbone: manumanu, paemanu.
colleague: hoa *N*.
collect: (kohi)kohi-a, huihui-a, raapoi-a.
college: kaareti.
collide: tuutuki (tuu-kia).
colonel: kaanara *N*.

colony: koroni *N*.
colour: kara *N*.
comb: heru-a, wani-a.
come: haere mai.
comely: huumaarire.
comfort: oranga ngaakau.
command: tono-a, whakahau-a.
commensurate with: rite ki.
commerce: hoko taonga.
commercial world: ao hokohoko.
committee: komiti.
common (ritually): noa *A*.
communicate with: paa ki.
compact: whaaiti *A*, hiato.
companion: hoa, takataapui.
company: kamupene *N*, tira *N*, ope *N*, roopuu *N*.
compare: whakataurite-a.
comparison: whakatauritenga.
compartment: tiriwaa.
compass: kaapehu *N*.
compassion: aroha-tia.
compel: aa-ia.
compensate: whakaea-tia, utu-a.
compensation (money): moni whakaea.
competition: whakataetae.
competitor: kai-whakataetae.
complain: amuamu-tia, haku-a.
complete, be complete: oti *P*, whakaoti-a, tutuki *A*, rite *A*.
comprehend: moohio-tia.
conceal: huna-a, whakangaro-mia, kuhu-a.
conceited: whakahiihii.
conceive (become pregnant): hapuu *A*.

concert: koonohete *N*, poo ngahau.
conciliate: whakamaarie-tia, here-ngia.
conclude: whakamutu-a, whakaoti-a.
conclusion: mutunga *N*, otinga *N*, taunga *N*.
condemn: whakahee-ngia.
conditions (of contract, etc.): tikanga *N*.
conditions (circumstances): aahuatanga *N*.
condom: puukoro (ure).
conduct (a case, business): whakahaere-a.
conduct (lead): arahi-na, arataki-na.
confess: whaaki-na, taapae.
confidence: whakamanawa, maia.
confine: aapiti-ria.
confirmed: mau *P*, tuuturu.
confounded: hane-a, poorararuru *A*.
confront: (tuu) haangai.
confuse *v.t.***:** whakapooheehee-tia, whakararu-a.
confused: pooauau *A*, pooheehee *A*, pooraru(raru) *A*.
congeal: (to)toka.
conger: ngooiro.
congregate: (hui)hui-a, whakamine.
connect: hono-a.
conscience: hinengaro.
conscious: moohio-tia, maatau-ria, mahara-tia.
consecrate: whakatapu-a.

consent: whakaae-tia, pai-
ngia(ki).
consequence: tukunga iho, hua.
consider: (aata) whakaaro-tia.
consolation: oranga ngaakau,
whakamaarietanga *N*.
conspicuous: koohure-a.
constable: piriihimana *N*.
constant: puumau, tuuturu.
constrict: nanati (naatia),
nonoti (nootia), kukuti
(kuutia), whakawhaaiti-tia.
consume, consumed: pau *P*,
whakapau-ngia, peto *P*.
contaminate: taahawahawa-tia,
whakaparu-a.
contend: (to)tohe-a,
tautohe-tia.
content: tatuu, naa.
contents: ngaa mea o roto.
contentious: tohetohe,
tautohetohe.
continuation: roanga *N*.
contract *v*.: huru-a, huupeke,
hukihuki.
contradict: whakahee-ngia.
contribute: hoomai, hoatu,
tuku-a.
control *n*.: tikanga *N*, mana *A*.
control *v*.: whakahaere-a.
convalescent: maatuutuu.
converse: koorerorero.
convert: kawe kee, huri kee,
whakatahuri-ngia, riro kee.
convey: (*See* carry).
conveyance: waka *N*.
convolvulus: poohue *N*.
convulsion: hukihuki, hukeke.
cook *v*.: tao-na, tahu-na,
whakamaaoa-tia, koohue-tia.

cook *n*.: tuumau, kuki.
cooked: maoa *P*.
cookhouse: kaauta *N*.
cool *a*.: hauhau *A*, maataotao
A, hauangi *A*.
cool *v*.: whakamaataotao-ria,
whakakoopeke-tia.
co-operate, -tion: mahi tahi.
cop (traffic): keehua *N*.
copious: nui *A*, ranea *A*.
copper: kapa.
copulate: ai-tia.
copy *v*.: mea kia rite *N*.
co-ordinate: whakarite-a.
cord: aho *N*.
core: uho *N*.
cork *v*., *n*.: puru-a, kooke *N*.
corn: kaanga *N*.
corn (fermented): kaanga wai,
kaanga koopiro.
corner: kokonga, koko, koki,
kopa.
cornflakes: kaanga rere,
kaanga kao.
corpse: tuupaapaku *N*.
correct: tika *A*, tootika,
whakatika-ia.
correspond (match): rite *A*,
whakarite-a.
cost: utu-a.
cough: mare, wharo.
council: kaunihera *N*,
ruunanga.
count: (ta)tau-ria.
countenance *n*.: mata *N*,
kanohi *N*.
counter-claim (legal): keehi
taawari *N*.
country: whenua *N*.
courage: toa *A*, maaia *A*.

court *v.*: whakaipoipo, aruaru wahine.
court *n.*: kooti.
courtyard: marae *N.*
cousin (boy of girl): tungaane.
cousin (girl of boy): tuahine (*pl.* tuaahine).
cousin (in English sense): kaihana *N.*
cousin (older of same sex): tuakana (*pl.* tuaakana).
cousin (younger of same sex): teina (*pl.* teeina).
covenant: kawenata *N.*
cover, covered: hiipoki-na, uwhi-a, taupoki-na, kapi *P.*
covet: popono, taiapo-tia.
cow: kau *N.*
cowardly, cowardice: taawiri.
crab: paapaka.
crack, cracked: pao-a, patoo-hia, kooara *A.*
crack (make cracking sound): patatee, patee.
crack (as lice with fingernail): tiipaki.
cracked: ngaatata *P.*
crackling (pork): pakapaka *N.*
crafty: maminga-tia.
cram: whakakikii, apu-a.
cramped: matangerengere.
crane (blue): matuku *N.*
crane (white): kootuku *N.*
crash: wheoro, paora-tia.
crave: hiahia-tia, piirangi-tia.
crawl: ngaoki, ngooki, ngoi.
crayfish: kooura.
crazy: poorangi-tia.
creak: koongangi, kekee.
cream: kiriimi.

creased: kopakopa.
create: hanga-a.
creed *n.*: (tuumomo) whakapono.
creek: (pekanga) awa, wai.
creep: ngaoki, ngooki, whakapapa.
crevice: kapiti *A.*
cricket (game): kirikiti.
cricket (insect): pihareinga *N*, rirerire.
crime: hara *A.*
criminal: tangata hara.
cripple: hauaa *A.*
criticise: whakahee-ngia.
crooked: hape *A*, noni, nuke, hake, parori.
crop (cut short): mutumutu-a, poro-a, kutikuti.
cross *v.*: whiti-a, whakawhiti-a.
cross *n.*: riipeka-tia.
cross (angry): pukuriri.
crossroad: pekanga, ara riipeka.
crouch: tuururu, noho koromeke.
crow *n.*: kookako *N.*
crowbar: koropaa.
crowd *v.*: inaki-tia, aapuru-a, taamuimui, popoo.
crowd *n.*: huihuinga, whakaminenga.
crowded: apiapi, koopipiri.
crown: karauna *N*, karaaone *N.*
crown (of head): tipuaki, tumuaki.
crucify: riipeka-tia.
crumb: kongakonga.
crumbled: ngawhara *A*, ngahoro *P.*

crupper: karapa, koropaa.
crush, crushed: koopenupenu, maruu *P*, pee *A*, whakapee, mongamonga.
cry: tangi-hia, auee-tia.
cuckoo (shining): piipiiwharauroa *N*.
cultivate: ngaki-a.
cultivation: mahinga kai.
cunt: teke *N*, tore *N*, teme *N*.
cup: kapu *N*.
cupboard: kaapata *N*.
cure *v.*: whakaora-ngia.
cure *n.*: rongoaa *N*.
cured: ora *A*.
curl *v.* **(of wave):** kapukapu, wharewhare.
curl (of hair): koromenge(menge).

curl (of smoke): riporipo.
curly: kapu.
curly (distinct curls): kapu maawhatu, koromengemenge.
curly (wavy): kapu mahora.
curly (woolly): kapu piripiri.
current: au *N*, ia *N*, roma *N*.
curse: kanga-a, kohukohu.
curtain: aarai-tia.
curved: tiiwhana.
custom: ritenga *N*, tikanga *N*.
cut: kokoti (kootia), haehae-a, tapahi-a, ripi-a, tope-a, poro-a.
cuttlefish: wheke *N*.

D

dagger: oka-ina.
daily: i teenei raa, i teenei raa.
dam *n.*: matatara.
damaged: kino *A*.
damp: maakuukuu *A*, haumaakuu.
dance: haka-a, kanikani.
dandle: poipoi-a.
dangle: tarewa, taaepaepa.
dare: maaia *A*.
dark: poouri, poo-ngia, hinapoouri *A*, parauri, waitutu *A*, kaahiwahiwa *A*.
dart *v.*: kookiri-tia, wero-hia.
dart *n.*: pere, tiimata, teka.
dash: aki-na, taa-ia.

date (time): raa *N*.
date of birth: raa whaanau.
daub: pani-a.
daughter: tamaahine.
daughter-in-law: hunaonga.
dawdle: aweke, whakananawe tarioi.
dawn: atatuu, atapoo, hii te ata.
day: raa, rangi, awatea, ao.
daylight: awatea *A*.
dazzled: koorekoreko.
deacon: riikona.
dead: mate *A*, hemo *A*.
deaf: turi *A*.
dear (expensive): utu nui.

dear (loved): aroha-ina.
debt: nama *N*.
decayed: pirau *A*.
deceive: tinihanga-tia, hangarau, nukarau-tia, maminga-tia.
December: Tiihema *Pnl*.
decide: whakarite-a, whakatau-a.
decision: whakatau.
declare: koorero-tia.
decrease: iti haere, whakaheke-a.
deep: hoohonu *A*.
deer: tia *N*.
defeat *n.*: hinganga *N*.
defeated: hinga *P*, mate *A*.
defect: kino *A*, koha *N*, mate *A*.
defend: wawao.
defy: whakatara-a, whakatuma.
degenerate: heke te tupu.
delay: whakaroa-tia.
delighted: aahuareka, wehi i te rekareka, hari *A*.
delirious: poorangi-tia, haawata.
deliver: whakaora-tia.
deluded: hewa, pohewa, pooheehee.
demand: tono-a.
demolish: whakahoro-a, whakahinga-ia.
denture: pereti niho.
deny: whakakaahore-tia.
depart, departed: haere atu, riro *P*.
deposit (part payment): moni maaka.

depreciation (of value): hekenga waariu.
deputy: teputi *N*, tuarua *N*.
descend: heke.
descendant: uri *N*, aitanga *N*.
descent: heketanga *N*.
describe: whakaatu i te aahua.
desecrate: whakanoa-tia.
desert: kooraha.
deserted: mahue *P*.
desire: hiahia-tia (ki), piirangi-tia, koro-a, korou-tia, uara-tia, mate-a, wawata-tia, minamina.
desolate: takoto kau.
desperate, desperation: whakamoomori.
despise: whakahaawe-a.
destroy, destroyed: ngaro *A*, huna-ia, takakino-tia, whakamootii.
detain: (pu)puri-tia.
detest: whakarihariha, whakahouhou.
devil: rewera.
devour: kai-nga.
dew: haukuu, toomairangi.
diamond: taimana *N*.
diarrhoea: tikotiko.
die: mate, hemo.
differ: puta kee.
difficult: uaua *A*.
dig: keri-a, ngaki-a.
dig (up): hauhake-tia.
dignity: aahua rangatira, tuu rangatira.
diligent: mamahi, ahuwhenua, puku mahi.
diminished: iti iho.
diocese: piihopatanga *N*.

dip: tou-a.
direct (manage): whakahaere-a.
direct (point out): tohutohu.
direct (straight): tika *A*, tootika *A*.
directions: tohutohu (ara).
dirge: apakura *N*.
dirt: paru *A*.
disagreeable: weriweri, whakarihariha.
disappear, disappeared: ngaro *A*, toremi *A*, nunumi *P*.
disapprove: whakakino-tia.
disarrange: whakatoohenehene.
disaster: aituaa *A*.
disbelieve: whakahori-a, whakateka.
discern: kite-a.
disciple: akonga *N*, tauira *N*.
disclose: whakakite-a, whakapuaki-na, whakaaturia, whaaki-na.
discomfort: huuhi.
discover: kite-a, hura-hia.
discuss: aata koorero, huri, whiriwhiri.
discs (agricultural): kiiwha.
disdain: whakaparahako-tia.
disease: mate *A*.
disembowel: tuaki-na.
disentangle: (we)wete-kia.
disgust: whakarihariha, whakahouhou, moorikarika.
dish: riihi *N*.
dishevelled: huutoitoi, tuuheihei.
dishonest: tinihanga-tia, hiianga.
disinclination: ngaakaukore.
disinter: hahu-a.

dislike: kino *A*, whakakino-tia.
dismiss: tono atu.
disobedient: turi *A*.
disobey: takahi te kupu.
disorderly: takoto kee.
disparage: ha(ni)hani.
dispersed: marara *P*.
display: whakakite-a, whakaari-a.
dispute: tautohetohe, ngangare.
disquieted: aawangawanga, pairi.
dissimulate: tuapeka.
distant, distance: tawhiti *A*, mamao *A*, paamamao *A*.
distasteful: kawa *A*.
distortion: rori-a.
distortion (of face): ngangahu.
distract, distracted: whakaware-a, ware-a.
distress, distressed: poouri *A*, mate *A*, aawangawanga *A*.
distribute: tohatoha, tuwha-ia.
district: takiwaa *N*.
disturb: whakararu-a.
disturbance: ngangau.
ditch: waikeri, awakeri.
dive: ruku-hia.
divide: (wehe)wehe-a, (waa)waahi-a.
division: waahanga *N*, kotinga *N*.
dizzy, dizziness: aanini *A*.
do: mea-tia.
doctor: taakuta *N*, rata *N*.
doctrine: akoranga, whakaakoranga *N*.
dodge: kootiti haere, whetau, kooriparipa.
dog: kurii, kiirehe.

dogfish: mangoo *N*.
donation: koha *N*.
donkey: kaaihe.
door: tatau, kuaha, whatitoka.
dot: tongi.
double: taapara, rererua,
　paparua, puu.
doubt, doubtful: rua,
　rapurapu, raupeka.
doubtless: kaaore e kore, e kore
　e kore.
down payment: moni maaka.
doze: (ne)newha.
drag: too-ia, kukume
　(kuumea).
dragonfly: kapo-wai *N*,
　tarakena *N*.
drain: awakeri, whakatahe-a,
　waikeri-ngia.
draughts: muu.
draw: (tuhi)tuhi-a.
drawer: toroa *N*.
dread, dreadful: wehi *A*,
　mataku.
dream: moemoeaa *N*, moe-a.
dredge: kaarau *N*.
dress *v.*, *n.*: kaakahu-ria,
　whakaakakahu-ria.
drift: tere *A*.
driftwood: taawhaowhao *N*.
drill (tool): wiri.

drink: inu-mia.
drip: tu(ru)turu.
drive: aa-ia.
drive (a vehicle): taraiwa-tia.
drizzle: koonehunehu *N*.
drop *v.*: makere *A*,
　maaturuturu.
drop *n.*: pata.
drowned: toremi *P*, toromi *P*.
drowsy: hiamoe, momoe.
drug: rongoaa *N*.
drug (mind changing): mea
　whakahaurangi.
drum: taramu *N*.
drunk: haurangi *A*.
dry: maroke *A*,
　whakamaroke-tia.
dumb: wahanguu.
duck *v.t.*: rumaki-na.
duck *n.*: rakiraki *N*, paarera *N*.
duck (blue): whio.
duck (paradise): puutangitangi.
dung: tuutae *N*.
dungarees: taangari *N*.
durable: ora roa.
dust: nehu, puehu.
Dutch: Tatimana *N*.
dwell: noho-ia.
dwelling: whare *N*.
dwelling-place: kaainga *N*.
dwindle: iti-haere.

E

each: teenei . . . teenei, teenaa
　. . . teenaa, teeraa . . . teeraa.
eager: kaikaa, ngaakau-nui.

ear: taringa.
early: moata *A*.
earth: ao *N*.

earth (dirt): oneone *N*, paru *A*.

earth up: ahuahu.

earthquake: ruu.

eased (of pain): mauru *P*.

east: raawhiti *N*.

Easter: Te Aranga *N*.

easy: ngaawari, waingoohia.

eat: kai-nga.

eat (ravenously): kaihoro.

eat (raw): ota.

eat (scraps): hamuhamu.

ebb: timu *A*.

ebb-tide: tai timu.

echo: paoro, pari kaarangaranga.

eddy: ripo.

edge (of a cutting instrument): koinga *N*, mata.

educate: whakaako-ria.

education: mahi whakaako.

eel: tuna *N*.

eel (conger): ngooiro.

eel-pot: hiinaki.

effective: mana *A*.

effort: kaha *A*, uaua.

egg: hua manu, heeki *N*.

eight: waru *A*.

eighteen: tekau maa waru.

eighth: tuawaru.

eighty: waru tekau.

eject: pana ki waho, pei-a.

elated: koa, hari *A*.

elbow: tuketuke-a, whatianga *N*.

elder *n*.: kaumaatua-tia.

elevate, elevated: whata-a, haapai-nga, tairanga *A*, whakatairanga-tia.

eleven: tekau maa tahi.

elsewhere: ki teetahi waahi, ki hea raanei.

emaciated: kiko kore, tuuwai, tuupuhi.

embalm (mummify): whakapakoko-tia.

embankment: maioro *N*.

embark: eke-a, eke-ngia.

embellish: whakapaipai, raakei-tia.

embers: ngaarehu *N*, waro.

embrace: awhi-tia.

emerge: puta *A*, ea *P*.

emetic: rongoaa whakaruaki.

emigrate: heke-a.

employ: whakamahi-a.

employer: paahi *N*, kaiwhakamahi *N*.

empty: takoto kau.

enable: whakakaha, whakamana-a.

encampment: puni, pahii *N*.

encircle: hao-a, koopani-a, karapoti *A*.

enclosure: raaihe *N*.

encourage: whakamanawa, akiaki, whakahauhau.

encumber, encumbered: whakawheruu-tia, raru *A*, wheruu.

encumbrance: taawekaweka.

end: pito *N*, mutunga *N*, otinga *N*.

endeavour *v*.: tohe, puta te uaua.

ended: mutu *P*.

endless: mutunga-kore.

enemy: hoariri *N*.

energetic: hihiri.

energy: ngoi, kaha *A*, uaua *A*,
  korou.
enfeeble, enfeebled:
  whakangoi-kore, ruhi *A*.
engine: miihini, mihiini.
England: Ingarangi *L*.
Englishman: Ingarihi *N*.
enlarge: whakanui-a.
enmity: mauaahara.
ennoble: whakarangatira,
  whakanui-a, rangatira *A*.
enough: ka nui.
enough!: Heoi anoo!
enquire: ui-a, paatai-a.
entangle, entangled: aarau,
  hiirau-tia, whiwhi.
enter: tomo-kia, uru, kuhu-a.
entertain: whakangahau-tia.
entertainment: mahi
  whakangahau.
entice: paatari(tari), poa(poa).
entrails: wheekau *N*, ngaakau
  N.
entrance: tomokanga *N*,
  wahapuu *N*, kuu(w)aha *N*.
envelop: koopaki-na.
envelope: koopaki.
envious: puuhaehae, harawene.
epidemic: mate urutaa.
episcopate: piihopatanga *N*.
equal: rite *A*, hoorite *A*.
erect *v.*: whakatuu-ria.
error: hee *A*.
escape, escaped: puta *A*,
  pahure *A*, ora *A*.
establish: whakanoho-ia,
  whakapuumau-tia.
eternal: mutunga kore.
evaluate: titiro ki te pai, kino
  raanei.

evaporate: mimiti *A*.
evening: ahiahi *A*.
ever *a.*: tonu ake.
everlasting: mau tonu.
every: katoa *N*.
evidence: koorero e paa ana ki.
evident: maarama *A*.
evil: kino *A*.
exact: tino *N*.
exalt: whakanui-a.
examination: whakamaatautau.
examine: maatakitaki, titiro
  (tiro-hia), titiro whakatau.
example: tauira *N*.
excellent: rawe *A*.
excessive: nui *A*.
exchange: hoko-na.
exchange of ideas:
  whakawhitiwhiti whakaaro.
excite: whakapaataritari,
  whakaongaonga.
exert oneself: tohe, whakauaua.
exhaust *v.*: whakapau-ngia.
exhausted (expended): pau *P*.
exhausted (of land): huuiki *A*.
exhaustion: ngenge *A*.
exhort: whakahau-a.
exhume: hahu-a.
expect: tuumanako-tia, tatari
  (taaria).
expel: pei-a, pana-a,
  tuu(w)hiti-tia.
experienced: maatanga,
  tautoohito.
expertise: waia.
explain: whakamaarama-tia.
explode: papaa, pahuu.
explore: toro-na, hoopara
  whenua.
exposed: puare *A*.

extend (as arms): totoro (torohia).
extend (lengthen): whakaroa-tia.
extension cord: waea whakaroa.
extensive: whaarahi, whaanui.
extent: roanga *N*, nuinga *N*.
exterminate: whakamootii, whakangaro-mia.
extinguished: poko *A*, pirau *A*, weto *P*.
extol: whakahirahira.
extremity: pito *N*, matamata *N*.
exultant: koa *A*.
eye: kanohi *N*, karu *N*, mata *N*.
eyeball: whatu.
eyebrow: kape, tukemata *N*, pewa.
eyelash: kamo.
eyelid: rewha.

F

fable: koorero tara, koorero pakiwaitara.
face *v.*: anga ki, aro ki.
face *n.*: mata *N*, kanohi *N*.
facing boards on gable of house: maihi *N*.
factory: wheketere *N*.
faded: haatea *A*, maawhe *A*.
faint *a.*: maiangi *A*.
faint-hearted: mooteatea, ngaakau taiatea.
fair (complexion): kiritea, kiri maa.
fair (weather): paki *A*.
faith, have faith: whakapono-a.
faithful: pono *A*.
fall: hinga *A*.
fall (dropped): makere *A*, marere *A*.
fall (to one's lot): taka ki.
fallow: paatohe.
false: teka, hori, parau *A*.
falsify: aweke-tia.
fame: rongo, rongonui.
familiarised: taunga-tia, wai-a.
family: whaanau.
famine: waa kai kore.
famous: ingoa nui, rongo nui, aranga *A*.
fan *v.*: koowhiuwhiu.
fantail: piiwaiwaka, piirairaka, piiwakawaka, tiirairaka.
far away: i/kei tawhiti.
farewell!: haere raa!.
farm: paamu *N*.
farmer: kaimahi-paamu *N*.
farther: koo atu.
fashion: whakaahua-tia, hanga-a, tarai-a.
fast (fixed): uu *A*, mau *P*, tina *P*.
fast *a.* **(quick):** tere *A*, kakama *A*, hohoro.
fast *v.*: noho puku.
fasten: whakauu-ngia, whakamau-a, whakapiri, titi-a.
fat *a.*: moomona *A*.

fat *n.*: ngako *N*, hinu *N*.
father: paapaa, matua taane.
father-in-law: hungawai *N*,
   hungarei *N*.
fathom: maaroo *A*.
fatigued: ngenge *A*, maauiui *A*.
fault: hee *A*, hapa *A*.
fear: wehi *A*, mataku *A*.
feast: haakari.
feather(s): hou, huruhuru, piki.
February: Pepuere *Pnl*.
fee: utu.
feeble: ngoikore, iwikore.
feed *v.*: whaangai-a.
feel (sense): rongo-hia.
feel (touch): whaawhaa-ria.
fell: tua-ina, tope-a.
fellow: korokee, maaia,
   autaaia.
female (animal): uha, uwha.
female (human): wahine.
feminism: tohe i te mana
   wahine.
feminist: kai-tohe i te mana
   wahine.
fence: taiepa, taiapa.
fender (of fire): aarai ahi.
fern (bracken): rarauhe *N*.
fern (tree-fern): mamaku *N*,
   wheekii *N*, ponga *N*,
   kaponga *N*.
**fernroot (edible rhizome of
   bracken):** aruhe *N*.
fertile land: whenua moomona.
fester: tongako.
fetch: tiki (tiiki-na), kawe-a.
fetid: piro *A*, haunga *A*.
fever: kiri kaa, piiwa.
few: torutoru, ouou.
fibre: kaka, weu.

field: paatiki, taiapa.
field (cultivated): maara *N*.
fierce: riri, nanakia.
fifteen: tekau maa rima *A*.
fifth: tuarima.
fifty: rima tekau.
fig: piki *N*.
fight: whawhai-tia (ki), riri
   (riiria), parekura *N*.
figure: whika *N*.
figure-head: tauihu *N*.
file (implement): whairuru *N*.
file (row): tira.
fill: whakakii, utu-a, whawhao,
   whaaona.
fill a vacancy: whakakapi-a.
fillip: koropana.
film (movie): pikitia.
filth: paru *A*.
fin: tira.
fin (dorsal): urutira.
fin (of flying fish, gurnard):
   paihau.
fin (throat): pakihawa.
fin (ventral): hawa.
find: kite-a.
fine (of thread): tarapii.
fine (weather): paki *A*.
finger-nail: maikuku *N*,
   matikuku *N*.
finish (cease): whakamutu-a.
finish (complete): whakaoti-a.
finish (use up): whakapau-a.
finished (ceased): mutu *P*.
finished (completed): oti *P*.
finished (used up): pau *P*.
fire: ahi *N*, kaapura *N*.
fire (a gun): pupuhi (puuhia).
firewood: wahie *N*, peka *N*.
firm: uu, mau *A*, taketake, kita.

first *a.*: tuatahi.
first *ad.*: maatua, wawe *P.*
first-born: maataamua *N.*
first-fruits: tamaahu,
  tuuaapora.
fish *v.* **(with line):** hii-a.
fish *n.*: ika *N*, ngohi *N.*
fish (bob for eels): toitoi.
fish (net): hao-a.
fish-hook: matau *N*, piihuka *N.*
fishing-line: aho *N.*
fishing-rod: matire.
fit (physically): whiti, ora *A*,
  kaha *A.*
five: rima *A.*
fix (make fast): whakauu-ngia.
fix (make good):
  whakapai-ngia.
fixed (made fast): uu *P*, mau *P.*
flabby: ngehengehe,
  ngohengohe.
flaccid: taroma.
flag: kara *N*, haki *N.*
flail: karawhiu-a.
flame: mura.
flap (in wind): taareparepa.
flap (of wings): kapakapa.
flash: hiko, rapa.
flat: papatahi, papa-tairite *A*,
  paaraharaha *A*, pararahi.
flatter: whakapatipati.
flavour *n.*: haa, reka *A.*
flawless: para-kore.
flax: harakeke *N*, koorari *N.*
flax (stalk): koorari *N.*
flay: tiihore-a.
flea: puruhi, keha *N*, tuiau *N.*
fleece: pirihoo *N.*
fleet (of vessels): kaupapa.
flesh: kikokiko.

flexible: piingore, ngohengohe,
  ngaawari *A.*
flight: rere.
flinch: kooemi.
fling: maka-a, whiu-a, akiri-tia.
flint: kiripaka, mataa *N.*
float, afloat: maanu *P*, rewa *P*,
  tere *A.*
float *n.*: poito, pouto *N.*
flock (of birds): pookai.
flock (of sheep): kaahui,
  maapu *N.*
flog: whiu-a, wepu-a.
flood: waipuke-tia.
floor: whoroa, kaupapa.
flounder *v.*: kowheta.
flounder *n.*: paatiki *N.*
flour: paraaoa *N.*
flow: rere *A*, paatere.
flower: puuaawai, putiputi *N.*
flute: puutorino *N*, kooauau *N.*
fly *v.*: rere, topa.
fly *n.*: ngaro, rango *N.*
fly (kite): whakaangi manu.
fly (sandfly): namu *N.*
flying fish: maaroro *N.*
foam: huka.
foaming: huhuka.
fog: kohu, puukohu *N.*
foiled: rahu-a, pare-a.
fold *v.*: taanumi,
  whakakopakopa-ia,
  koopake-tia.
fold *n.*: puukoru, whatianga *N.*
fold (hanging in folds):
  taakoru, haangorungoru.
follow: aru-mia, whai, whaai-a.
fondle: mirimiri,
  whakamaimoa.
food: kai-nga, oo *N*, oranga *N.*

foolish: kuuare, heahea, poorangi, wairangi.
foot: waewae *N.*
foot (measure): putu *N.*
football: hutupaoro *N.*
footprint: tapu(w)ae *N.*
forbid: whakakaahore-tia, whakakore, peehi-a, raahui-tia.
force, *n.*: kaha *A.*
force, come into: whai-mana.
force, driving: aainga *N.*
force open: koara-tia.
force (psychic): mana *A.*
ford *n.*: kauanga *N,* whakawhitinga *N.*
forearm: kikowhiti.
forehead: rae *N.*
foreigner: tauiwi, Paakehaa, raawaho.
foreleg: peke *N.*
forerunner: maataarere.
forest: ngahere *N,* ngaaherehere *N,* ngahengahe.
forget: wareware-tia (ki).
forgotten: wareware (i).
fork: paaoka *N,* whaaka *N,* maarau *N.*
fork (of a tree, path): pekanga *N.*
form *v.*: whakaahua-tia.
form *n.*: aahua, kaahua.
form (paper): pepa *N.*
former: too mua.
formerly: i mua, i namata.
fornicate, fornication: puuremu-tia, moe taahae.
forsake: whakarere, whakareere-a.

fort: paa *N.*
fortification: paa *N,* paa tuuwatawata.
forty: whaa tekau.
foster: whaangai-tia.
fosterchild: tamaiti whaangai, taurima, tamaiti atawhai.
foul (smelling): kerakera, piro *A.*
foul (broken rule): hara *A.*
four: whaa *A.*
fourteen: tekau maa whaa.
fowl: heihei *N,* piikaokao *N,* tiikaokao *N.*
fracture, fractured: pakau *P,* whati *P,* whawhati, whaatiia.
fragment: maramara, mea rikiriki.
fragrant, fragrance: kakara.
France, French: Wiiwii *N.*
fraud: tinihanga-tia.
freckle: ira.
freckled: kootiwhatiwha.
free (unoccupied): waatea *P.*
free (set free): whakatangatanga, tuku kia haere.
freedom (personal): mana tangata.
freezer: (pouaka) aihi *N.*
Frenchman: Wiiwii *N.*
frequent: hoki putuputu.
frequency (channel): ara, aratuku.
fresh: hoou *A.*
fresh (freshwater): wai maaori.
fresh (of vegetables): kaimata.
fret: koingo-tia.
Friday: Paraire *N.*
friend: hoa *N.*

fridge: pouaka maatao.
fright, frighten, frightened: mataku *A*, whakamatakuria, wehi *A*, whakawehi-a.
frivolous: hangahanga.
frog: poroka *N*.
front: mua *L*.
front (of person): aroaro.
frost: huka, hukapapa, haupapa, hauhunga.
froth: huka *N*.
fruit: hua (raakau) *A*.
fruitful: makuru.
fry: parai-tia.
frying-pan: parai, raupani.
fuchsia: kootukutuku *N*.
fulfilled: rite.

full: kii *P*.
full moon: Ooturu, Raakau-nui.
fullback: whurupeeke *N*.
fund: puutea moni.
fungus: harore, hawai, puutawa, keka, hakeke, tuutae keehua, (taringa) hookeke.
funnel: koorere.
furious: riri, pukuriri, kaarangirangi *A*.
further: ki koo atu.
fuse *n.*: wiki.
future: a muri, te waa ka heke mai nei, te waa kei te haere mai.

G

gable: ihi, maihi.
gain: whiwhi.
gale: aawhaa *N*, tuupuhi.
gallop: tupeke, takakii, kahaki.
gallop *v.t.*: whakakakahaki-tia.
game: taakaro, mahi ngahau.
gannet: takupu *N*.
gape: ko(w)hera.
garage: karaati *N*.
garden: maara *N*, kaari *N*, mahinga *N*.
garland: pare, tuupare.
garment: kaakahu *N*, kaka *N*, pu(w)eru *N*.
garment (old): karukaru, tawhetawhe.
gasoline: penehini *N*, hinu *N*.

gasp: kiha, kuha, tare.
gate: keeti *N*.
gateway: waharoa, kuu(w)aha.
gather (things): (kohi) kohi-a, whakamine-a.
gather (together, of people): hui(hui)-a.
gathered (together): ruupeke.
gather in (of a root crop): maea *A*, hauhake-tia.
gaze: maatakitaki, tirotiro, titiro whakatau, titiro maakutu.
gender: ira taane, wahine raanei.
genealogy: kaawai *N*, whakapapa, taatai-a.

general: tukipuu, tukupuu.
general, in: i toona tikanga.
generation: whakatupuranga *N*.
generous: atawhai, oha, marere (noa).
gentle: maahuu, maarire.
genuine: tupu, tuuturu.
Germany: Tiamana.
ghost: keehua *N*.
giddy, giddiness: aanini, anini.
gift: koha, mea tuku.
gill: piha, puha.
gimlet: wiri.
gird: whiitiki-tia.
girdle: whiitiki, taatua.
girl: kootiro *N*, koohine.
girth (harness): kati *N*.
give: hoomai, hoatu. (In classical Maori these words do not take passive suffixes though they are used in passive constructions.)
glad: hari *A*, koa-ina.
glare: kanapa.
glass: karaahe, karaehe, wini.
glean: hamu.
glide: tere *A*, roonaki, tiitipi.
glimmer: kaatoretore.
glisten: kanapa, wheriko.
gloomy: poouriuri, matapoouri.
glory: korooria *N*.
glow: puuhana.
glow-worm: puuraatoke.
glutton, gluttony: kaihoro, pukunui.
gnash: tetee.
gnat: waeroa *N*, naeroa *N*, naenae *N*.
gnaw: ngau-a.

go: haere-a atu, whanatu.
go (aside): peka.
go (round about): aawhio.
go (to and fro): koopikopiko.
goad: whakaongaonga.
goat: koati *N*, nanenane *N*.
goat (nanny): nanenane *N*, nanekoti *N*.
goblin: tupua, keehua, tuurehu *N*.
god: atua *N*.
godwit: kuaka *N*.
gold: koura *N*.
gone: riro *P*.
gone (all gone): pau *P*.
gone (for good): haere oti atu.
good: pai *A*.
goodbye (said by person going): e noho ra, hei konei ra.
goodbye (said by person staying): haere ra.
goods: taonga *N*, taputapu *N*.
goose: kuihi *N*.
gooseberry: kuihipere, kuupere.
gorge *v.*: apu-a, kai apu, kai apo.
gorge *n.*: kapiti.
gospel: rongo pai.
gossip: pakitara, tuutara.
got, gotten: riro i.
gourd: hue, wenewene.
gourd (calabash): tahaa *N*, kiiaka, ipu *N*.
govern: whakahaere tikanga.
grace: aroha noa.
graft: hono-a.
grain (in timber): kakano.
grain (seed): kaakano.
grandchild: mokopuna.

grandfather, grandmother:
tupuna, tipuna (*pl.* tuupuna,
tiipuna).
grant (monetary): karaati *N*,
moni tuku.
grape: kerepi *N*.
grapnel: kaarua.
grasp: tango-hia, mau-ria.
grass: karaaihe *N*, paatiitii *N*,
tarutaru *N*.
grasshopper: koowhitiwhiti,
maawhitiwhiti *N*,
paakauroharoha *N*.
grate: roroi.
gratified: maaha *P*, naa.
grave *n.*: rua *N*, poka.
gravel: kirikiri *N*.
gravy: wairanu.
grayling: upoko-roro.
graze: wani-a, koonihi.
grease *n.*: hinu *N*.
great: nui *A*, rahi *A*.
greedy: kaihoro, pukukai.
green (colour): kaakaariki.
green (of foliage): matomato,
maaota.
green (of fruit): mata, ota,
kaimata.
greenstone: pounamu *N*.
greet: mihi-a, poowhiri-tia.
grey (hair): hina, hinahina.
grey warbler: riroriro *N*.
grief: poouri *A*.
grill *v.*: hunuhunu-a, tunutunu-a.

grind (in mill): huri-hia.
grind (on a stone): oro-hia.
grindstone: hoanga *N*.
groan: auee, aurere.
groove: awaawa, haehae.
grope: whaawhaa haere.
groper: (w)haapuku.
ground: whenua *N*, oneone *N*.
ground (of quarrel, etc.): papa,
take.
grove: uru, motu, oro.
grow: tupu-ria.
grub: tunga, huhu *N*.
grumble: amuamu, hakuhaku,
wene.
grunt: ngunguru.
guard: tiaki-na.
guest: manuhiri *N*.
guide *v.*: arahi-na.
guide *n.*: kai-arahi.
gull: karoro *N*.
gulp: horo-mia.
gum: kaapia *N*.
gumboot: kamupuutu.
gums: tako, pae niho.
gun: puu.
gun (shotgun): puu hoota, puu
kariri.
gunpowder: paura.
gunwale: niao *N*.
gurgle: kokoo.
gurnard: kumukumu *N*.
gush: hiirere.
guts: wheekau *N*.

H

habit: ritenga *N*.
hack *v.*: tapahi-a.
hacksaw: kani maitai.
had (*past possession*): i whai-,
 i whiwhi.
had (*past perfect tense marker*):
 kua.
Hades: Te Poo.
hail *v.*: karanga-tia.
hail *n.*: ua nganga, ua whatu.
hair (of body, of animal, in
 general): huruhuru.
hair (of head): makawe (used in
 plural only), huruhuru.
half: haawhe-tia.
halfcaste: haawhe kaaehe *N*.
halftime: haawhe-taaima.
hallow: whakatapu-a.
halo: awheo.
halt: tuu.
Hamilton: Haamutana *L*.
hammer: hama, tuki.
hand: ringaringa *N*.
handful: kapunga *N*.
handkerchief: aikiha *N*,
 paakete *N*.
handle *v.*: (na)nao-mia, rarau,
 whaawhaa-ria.
handle *n.*: puritanga *N*, kawe,
 kakau *N*.
handsome: pai *A*, aataahua *N*.
hang, be hanging: taairi, iri-a,
 taarewa, tare.
hang (back): taawhitaawhi,
 toomuri.
hang (in folds): haangorungoru,
 pookurukuru.

hang (something): whakataairi,
 whakairi-a.
happen: tuupono.
happy: hari *A*, koa *A*.
hard: maaroo *A*, pakeke *A*,
 pakari *A*.
hard-case: haatakeehi,
 haarikeehi, nanakia *A*.
hard-working: mamahi,
 pukumahi.
hare: hea.
harm: kino *A*.
harp: haapa *N*.
harpoon: haeana raati.
harrow (scarifier): karawhaea,
 haro (rakaraka).
harrow (disc): kiiwhi, kiiwha.
harvest (time): hauhakenga,
 kotinga, ngahuru *N*.
has (possesses): whai-, whiwhi.
has (*perfect tense marker*): kua.
hasten: hohoro, whakahohoro.
hasty: hohoro, poorangi.
hat: pootae-a.
hatch: pao.
hatchet: paatiitii *N*, toki *N*.
hate: kino, whakakino,
 mauaahara.
haughty: whakahiihii,
 whakakake, ihu matiti.
haul: too-ia, kukume
 (kuumea).
haunt: kuku-a.
have (possess): whai-, whiwhi.
have (*perfect tense marker*):
 kua.
hawk: kaahu *N*.

hawk (sparrowhawk): kaarearea *N*.

haystack: taake hei.

haze: rehu, kohu.

head: upoko *N*, maatenga *N*, maahunga *N*, pane *N*.

head (back of): koohamo, koopako *N*.

head (forehead): rae *N*.

head (of a nail): peru *N*.

head (of a river): hiku-awa.

head (of a tree): kaauru *N*.

head (skull): angaanga *N*.

head (top of): tipuaki *N*, tupuaki *N*, tumuaki *N*.

headache: a(a)nini, ngaahoahoa, paahoahoa.

headland: rae, kuurae, more.

heal: whakaora, whakamahu.

healed: ora *A*, mahu *A*.

health: ora *A*, oranga *N*.

heap, heaped up, heap up: puu, puuranga-tia, apu-ria, ahuahu, tuuaahu, puukai-tia, taapukepuke *A*.

hear: rongo-hia (rangona).

heart (anatomical): manawa *N*.

heart (card suit): haate *N*.

heart disease: mate manawa.

heartburn: poho ngawhaa.

heat: wera *A*, paawera, mahana *A*.

heaven: rangi *N*.

heavy: taimaha *A*, toimaha *A*, taumaha *A*.

hectare: heketea.

heel: rekereke *N*.

height: tiketike, teitei.

helm: urungi-tia.

help: aawhina-tia.

hem (lower): remu.

hem (upper): kurupatu.

hen: heihei *N*, piikaokao *N*, tiikaokao *N*.

henceforth: a muri ake nei.

her: ia.

her, for: maana, moona.

herbs: otaota.

herd: kaahui, maapu *N*.

hereafter: a muri.

hereby: maa konei.

hermit crab: kaaunga.

heron (blue): matuku *N*.

heron (white): kootuku *N*.

herring: aua.

hers: naana, noona.

hew: hahau, haaua.

hiccough: tokomauri.

hide, be hidden: ngaro *P*, whakangaro-mia, huna, kuhu-a.

hide (skin): hiako.

high: tiketike, teitei, ikeike.

hill: puke.

him: ia.

him, for: maana, moona.

hinder: whakawheruu-tia, whakakooroiroi, whakararuraru.

hindrance: mea hei aarai.

hip: himu.

hips (hands on): ringa hope.

hire: riihi-tia.

his: naana, noona.

hiss: hii, huhuu.

hit, be hit: paa-kia, paa *P*, whara.

hither: mai *particle*.

hoarse: whango.

hoe (draw): karaone.
hoe (push): tipitipi.
hoist: (hu)huti-a.
hold *v.*: (pu)puri-tia, (ra)rawhi-a.
hold (of ship): riu.
hole: poka, puta, rua, koowhao.
holiday: hararei *Pnl.*
hollow *v.t.*: pokorua, wharemoa, whakakooruatia, whakapokorua-tia.
holy: tapu *A.*
home: kaainga *N,* kaainga tupu.
honey: miere, honi *N.*
honour: hoonore, whakahoonore-tia.
hook: matau, piihuka *N.*
hoop: korowhiti, piirori.
hop: hiiteki, hiitoko.
hop (of a bird): pekepeke.
hope: tuumanako-hia (ki).
horizon: pae, taaepaepatanga o te rangi, tuapae.
horn: haaona *N.*
horse: hooiho *N.*
hose: houhi *N.*
hospital: hoohipera *N,* hoohipere *N.*
host (many): mano, tini.
host (opp. of guest): tangata whenua.

hostilities: pakanga *N,* whawhai.
hot: wera *A,* kakaa.
hot (to the taste): puuhahana.
hotel: hootera *N,* paaparakauta *N.*
hour: haora.
house: whare *N.*
hover: whakatopa.
how: pee(w)hea-tia.
how many?: e (w)hia?
howl: tangi, auee, ngawii.
hug: tauapo-hia, tauawhi.
hum: tamumutia, mapu.
humorous: whakakata.
hunch (idea): whakaaro.
hunchback(ed): hake *A.*
hundred: rau *A.*
hundredweight: haanarete.
hunger, hungry: hiakai, hemo kai, mate kai.
hunt: whaiwhai, whakangau-a.
hurricane: tuupuhi.
hurry: poorangi, kaikaa, pootatu, puuaaritarita, kaihoro(horo), taataakino.
hurt *v.t.*: ngau, whakamamae-tia.
hurt (be hurt): whara *P.*
husband *n.*: taane *N.*
hush!: kaati! turituri! hoihoi!
husk *n.*: peha, koopaki.
hymn: hiimene *N.*

I

I, me: ahau, au, awau *Pnl.*
ice cream: aihikiriimi *N.*

idiot: poorangi, heahea.
idle: maangere *A.*

idol: whakapakoko.
ignorant: kuare.
ill: mate *A*, maauiui *A*.
ill-treat: tuukino-tia,
  takakino-tia.
illustrious: rongonui-tia, ingoa
  nui.
image: whakapakoko, tiki *N*.
imitate: whaaia, taawhai, kape.
immediately: (n)aianei tonu.
impatient: poorangi, taaruke,
  kaikaa, heemanawa.
important: nui *A*.
imposed upon: hiianga-tia.
imprison, be imprisoned: mau
  herehere.
improve *v.i.*: pai haere.
improve *v.t.*: whakapai-ngia.
inasmuch as: ina hoki.
inattentive: taringa turi, taringa
  muhukai.
incantation: karakia-tia.
inch: inihi *N*.
incite: akiaki,
  whakapaataritari,
  whakataritari.
inclination: hiahia, aro, aronui.
increase *v.*: nui haere.
India: Iinia *L*.
indistinct (of sight): rehu-a.
indistinct (of sound):
  hiirea(rea).
industrious: mamahi, ahu
  whenua, pukumahi.
ineffective (of people): hau-
  warea *A*.
inflamed (of eyes): toretore.
inflamed (of skin): puuhahana.
influence: mana *A*.
influenza: rewharewha, whuruu.

inform: whakaatu-ria, whaakii
  (whaakina).
information: whakaaturanga
  N.
inhabit: noho-ia.
initiate: whakatiimata-ngia.
injure, be injured: tuukino-tia,
  whara *A*.
injury: kino, tuukinotanga *N*.
ink: mangumangu.
inland: uta *L*, roto *L*.
inner man: Tama-roto *Pnl*.
inquire: paatai-a, ui-a.
insane: poorangi.
insect (grublike): ngaarara.
insect (other): peepeke.
insert: kuhu-a, whakauru-a.
inside: roto *L*.
insipid: haa-kore, waimeha-tia.
insolent: toro-ihi.
inspect: maataki(taki)-na, aata
  titiro (tirohia).
inspector: kai-tirotiro.
instigate: whakatuu-ria.
instruct: ako-na, whakaako-na.
instrument (musical): mea
  whakatangitangi.
insubordinate: tutuu.
insult: kanga-a.
intelligent: moohio-tia,
  maatau-ria.
intend: mea-tia.
intercede: inoi-a.
intercourse (sexual): mahimahi-
  a, onioni-tia, ai-tia.
interest (usury): itarete, hua o
  te moni.
interior: roto *L*.
interior (of a country): uta *L*.
interlace: kootui-a, rau(w)iri-tia.

intermission: paariiraatanga *N*.
intermittent: taamutumutu.
interpret: whakamaaori-tia.
interpreter: kai-whakamaaori
　N.
interrupt: aruaru.
interrupted: whati.
intertwine: rau(w)iri-tia.
interval: takiwaa *N*, waa *N*,
　tiriwaa *N*.
intestines: puku, wheekau *N*.
intonation: rangi (o te reo).
intoxicated: haurangi *A*.

invade: whakaeke-a.
invalid: tuuroro.
invert: huri kooaro.
Irish: Airihi.
iron: rino *N*, maitai *N*, haeana
　N.
irregular: whakahipahipa,
　koohikohiko.
irritating: maakatikati.
is: *See under* **be.**
island: moutere, motu.
Italy: Itaaria.
itch: rekareka *A*, ngaoko *A*.

J

jade: pounamu *N*.
jail: whare herehere.
jam: tiaamu *N*, haami *N*,
　haamu *N*.
January: Hanuere *Pnl*.
jaw: kau(w)ae *N*.
jealous, jealousy: (ha)hae,
　puuhaehae, harawene.
jeer: taunu.
jelly: purini korikori.
jellyfish: tepetepe.
jerk: taakiri-tia.
jersey: poraka.
jest: tinihanga-tia, hangarau.
jewel: rei, hakurangi.
Jew's harp: roria.
jib: (raa)ngongo-hau.
jingle: tatangi.

join: apiti-ria, hono-a,
　taapiri-tia.
joint (e.g. elbow): pona.
joist: kurupae.
jostle: tutetute, peipei.
journey: haere-a.
joy: hari *A*, koa *A*.
judge *v*.: whakawaa-kia.
judge *n*.: tiati *N*, kai-whakawaa
　N, kaiwhiriwhiri *N*.
jug: tiaka *N*, haaka *N*.
Jugoslav: Tararaa *N*.
juice: wai (reka).
July: Huurae *Pnl*.
jump: peke, tuupeke, moowhiti.
June: Huune *Pnl*.
jury: huuri *N*.
just *a*.: tika *A*.

K

keel: takere.
keep: (pu)puri-tia, tiaki-na.
keepsake: manatunga *N*, tohu
  aroha.
kerosene: karahiini *N*.
kettle: tiikera *N*.
kick: whana-a, kiki-a.
kidney: taakihi *N*, whatukihi
  N, whatukuhu *N*.
kill: patu-a.
kind, be kind: atawhai-tia.
kind *n.*: tuu,tuumomo, momo.
kindle: tahu-na.
kindred: whanaunga, huaanga.
king: kiingi *N*.
kingdom: kiingitanga *N*.
kingfish: haku, warehenga.
kingfisher: kootare *N*.
kiss: kihi-a.
kitchen: kiihini.
kitchen-hand: ringa wera.

kite: manu, paakau.
knead: poopoo, pokepoke,
  mekemeke.
knee: turi.
kneel: tuuturi.
knife: maripi *N*, naihi *N*.
knife (butcher): oka, puutia,
  puha.
knife (docking): naihi
  pokapoka.
knife (pocket): paakete naihi.
knob: puku.
knob (door-knob): puritanga.
knock: paatukituki, paakuru,
  paatootoo.
knot: pona.
knot (in wood): puku, pona.
know: maatau-ria, moohio-tia
  (ki), kite-a.
knowledge: maatauranga *N*.
knuckle: pona.

L

labour: mahi-a.
labour, be in:
  whakamamae-tia.
Labour (party): Reipa.
lace *v.*: (tui)tui-a, whaatui.
lacebark: houhere *N*, hoihere,
  houhi, houi.
ladder: arawhata *N*.
laden: (*See* load).
lady: wahine rangatira.

laity: reimana.
lake: roto *N*.
lamb: reme *N*.
lame: hauaa, kopa, hape *A*.
lament: auee, tangi-hia, mihi-a.
lamp: rama-a, raatana *N*, raiti.
lamprey: piharau.
lance: tao.
land *v.*: (whaka)uu-ngia ki uta,
  tau *P*.

land *n*.: whenua *N*.
land breeze: hau whenua,
  taawhenua.
landing place: uunga *N*,
  tauranga *N*.
landslip: horo.
language: reo *N*.
languid: ngoikore, iwikore.
lank: mahora.
lantern: raatana *N*.
lark: piihoihoi *N*.
large: nui, rahi *A*.
lash *v*.: whiu-a.
lash *n*.: (of a whip): kare.
lashing (binding): kaha,
  aukaha.
last: too-muri.
last (night): inapoo.
late: too-muri, tuureiti *A*.
latter: too muri.
laugh: kata-ina.
launch, launched (of a dart):
  kookiri-tia.
launch (a boat): whakamaanu-
  tia, whakarewa-tia.
launched (of a boat): maanu *P*,
  rewa *P*.
lavatory: whare paku, whare
  iti.
law: ture *N*.
lawful: tika.
lawyer: rooia *N*.
lay: whakatakoto-ria, waiho-
  tia, taapae.
lay (across): whakapae-a.
lay (one on another):
  whakapapa.
lay (out, of a corpse):
  whakaatamira-tia.
layer: whakapaparanga *N*.

layman: reimana *N*.
lazy: maangere *A*.
lead: arahi-na, arataki-na.
lead (metal): mataa *N*.
leader: kai-arahi *N*.
leaf: rau.
leaf (of a book): whaarangi.
leak: turuturu, koowhao *N*.
lean *v*.: wharara.
lean (against): wharara ki,
  whakawhirinaki-tia,
  whakaurunga-tia.
lean *n*.: tupuhi, tuu(w)ai *A*.
leap: peke, tuupeke-tia,
  rere-ngia.
learn: ako, aakona.
learner: akonga *N*.
lease: riihi.
least: te iti rawa.
leather: rera *N*, hiako (kau).
leave, be left: waiho-tia,
  whakarere-a, mahue *P*.
leek: riiki *N*.
left-handed: ringa mauii.
leg: waewae.
legend: koorero puurakau,
  koorero tupuna.
leggings: reekena *N*, reekene *N*.
lemon: reemana *N*.
lemonade: wai reemana.
length: roa *A*.
lengthen: whakaroa-tia.
leprosy: tuuwhenua, ngerengere
  N.
less: iti iho.
lessen: whakaiti-a.
let (down): whakaheke, tuku-a
  iho.
let (go): tuku-a kia haere.
let (lease, rent): reeti, riihi.

letter: pukapuka, reta *N*.
letter (of alphabet): reta *N*.
level: papatairite.
level (tool): reewara.
lever: hua.
liberal: atawhai, oha.
library: whare pukapuka.
licence: raihana.
lick: mitimiti, mitia.
lid: taupoki-na.
lie (down): takoto-ria.
lie (face down): taapapa-tia.
lie (on back): tiiraha.
lie *n*. (falsehood): parau, teka, tito, horihori.
lieutenant: ruutene *N*.
life: ora *A*.
lift: haapai-ngia, hiki-tia.
ligament: uaua.
light (not dark): maarama, ao, taiaoaho.
light (weight): maamaa *A*.
light (ignite): tahu-(n)a.
light *n*.: raiti, rama, raatana.
lighter (cigarette): puuahi *N*.
lightning: uira, kanapu, hiko.
like *a*.: rite.
like *v*.: aahuareka, aroha-tia, hiahia-tia, piirangi-tia, manako-tia.
like (be pleased with): aahuareka ki.
like how?: peehea-tia?
like this: peenei-tia.
like that: peenaa-tia, peeraa-tia.
liken: whakarite-a.
likeness: aahua *N*, ritenga *N*.
likewise: hoki.
lime: raima *N*.
limp *v*.: totitoti.

line (row): kapa.
line (fishing): aho, raina.
line (of print): raarangi.
lineage: kaawai, taatai tuupuna, whakapapa-tia.
linger: whakaroa-tia.
lintel: koorupe *N*, pare *N*.
lion: raiona *N*.
lip: ngutu *N*.
liquid: wai.
listen: whakarongo-hia (ki).
listless: ngoikore, iwikore, hau(w)area.
litter (stretcher): amo, kauamo.
little: iti *A*, pakupaku *A*, nohinohi *A*.
live (be alive): ora *A*.
live (dwell): noho-ia.
liver: ate *N*.
load: uta-ina, utanga *N*, kawenga *N*, wahanga *N*.
loaf (of bread): rohi (paraaoa).
loathsome: whakarihariha, weriweri, wetiweti, whakahouhou.
local community: iwi kaainga.
locality: waahi *N*.
lock (of door): raka.
lock (of hair): rino makawe.
locust: kihikihi, maawhitiwhiti *N*.
lofty: teitei, tiketike, ikeike.
log: poro raakau, rooku, tuuporo.
loiter: whakaroa-tia.
lolly: rare *N*.
lonely: mokemoke *A*.
long: roa *A*.
look: titiro (ki), tiro-hia, maatakitaki.

look (for): rapu-a, kimi-hia.
look (sideways): titiro kootaha, titiro tiitaha.
looking-glass: whakaata, mira *N*.
loop: koru.
looped: koopeti.
loose: matara, taangorongoro, tangatanga.
loosen: wewete, wete-kina.
lord: ariki *N*.
lost: ngaro *A*.
loud: tangi nui.
louse: kutu *N*.

love: aroha-ina (ki).
lover: whaiaipo, tau *N*.
love-song: waiata whaiaaipo, waiata aroha.
low: hakahaka, paapaku, hauraro.
low (of tide): timu, mimiti.
low (socially): ware, tuutuuaa.
lower *a*.: raro iho.
lower *n*.: too raro.
lucky: waimarie.
lunch: tina *N*.
lungs: pukapuka *N*.

M

macaroni: makaroni.
machine: miihini *N*, mihiini *N*.
mackerel: tawatawa *N*.
mad: poorangi.
maggot: iroiro *N*, keto *A*.
maggoty: keto *A*.
magnify: whakanui-a.
magnitude: nui *A*.
mail: meera.
mainland: tuawhenua *N*.
maize: kaanga *N*.
major: meiha *N*.
make: hanga-a.
Malaya: Mareia *L*.
male: taane *N*.
male (of animals): toa *A*, tame.
malice: mauaahara.
mallet: kuru, taa, tukituki.
maltreat: tuukino-tia.
man: tangata *N*. *(pl.* taangata) taane.

manage (be able): tae (taaea).
manage (conduct): whakahaere-a.
management committee: komiti whakahaere.
mange: waihakihaki.
mangrove: maanawa *N*.
manifest: maarama *A*.
manner: ritenga *N*, tikanga *N*, tuu.
manure: wairaakau, maniua, tongi.
many: maha *A*, tini *A*, huhua.
map: mapi *N*.
marble: maapere *N*, maaporo *N*.
March: Maaehe, *Pnl*.
margin: tapa.
mark: tohutohu.
marriage: maarenatanga *N*.

marrow: roro.
marrow (vegetable):
kamokamo.
marry: moe-a, maarena-tia,
whakamoe-a.
marsh: repo.
martingale: maatikere.
marvel: miiharo.
mash: koopenu(penu)-tia,
koonatu-a.
mashed: penupenu *A*.
mast: tira.
master: maahita *N*, rangatira
A.
mat (floor): whaariki-tia,
takapau, porera, taapau,
hiipora.
match: maati *N*.
match (contest): whakataetae.
mate: hoa.
matter (pus): pirau.
matter (subject): tikanga *N*.
matter (trouble): mate,
raruraru.
matter (what does it)?: hei aha?
mattock: maatiki, peeti.
mattress: matarehi *N*, peeti *N*.
mature: pakari *A*,
whakapakari.
maul *n.*: taa, mooro.
May: Mei *Pnl*.
me: ahau, au, awau.
mealy: maangaro *A*, maahunga
A.
meaning: tikanga *N*,
maaramatanga *N*.
measles: miitara *N*, miihara *N*.
measure: meehua, meiha.
meat: miiti *N*.
meddle: raweke-tia, rahurahu.

mediator: takawaenga, kai-
wawao *N*.
medicine: rongoa.
meditate: whakaaro-hia.
medium (spiritual): waka *N*.
meek: mahaki, waimarie *A*.
meet: tuutaki-na.
meet (of roads): puutahi.
melon: merengi *N*, kaakaariki
N.
melt: rewa *A*.
melt *v.t.*: whakarewatia,
whakarewa-ina.
member: mema *N*.
mend: tapi-a.
mend (of a net): taapuni-a.
menses: tahe.
mention: koorero-tia, kii-a,
mea-tia.
merchandise: taonga, taputapu.
merged: hanumi *P*.
merry: hari, koa.
mesh: mata, papa.
message: kupu *N*, koorero-tia.
messenger: karere *N*.
metal: meetara *N*.
meteor: matakookiri,
kootiritiri.
method: tikanga *N*.
metre: metre *N*.
middle: waenganui *L*, waenga
L.
midge: naonao *N*.
midnight: waenganui poo,
turuawepoo.
migrate, migration: heke-a.
mild: mahaki, ngaawari *A*.
mildew: hekaheka.
mile: maero *N*.
milk: miraka-tia, wai uu.

mill: mira *N.*
mind: hinengaro *N.*
mine *pron.*: naaku, nooku.
mineral pool: waiariki.
minister: minita *N.*
minority: itinga *N.*
minute: meneti *N.*
minute (small): iti rawa.
miracle: merekara.
mirror: whakaata, mira.
miscarriage: mate-roto, tahe, whakatahe.
mischief: porohianga, hiianga-tia.
misfortune: aituaa *A.*
misgiving: aawangawanga *A*, maanukanuka.
mislead: whakahee-ngia, whakapooheehee-ngia.
miss: hemo *P*, pahemo *P*, hipa.
missing: ngaro *P.*
missionary: mihinare *N.*
mist: kohu *N*, puunehu.
mistaken: hee *A*, pooauau *A*, pooheehee.
misty: puunehunehu.
mix: whakaranu-a, whakananu-a, whakahanumi-tia.
mixed: nanu *P*, ranu *P*, hanumi *P.*
moan: aurere.
moat: awa-keri, awa-kari, awa-mate.
mock: taunu.
model: tauira *N.*
moist: maakuu *A*, maakuukuu *A.*
moisten: whakamaakuukuu-tia.
molar (tooth): niho puu.
mole: iraira.

molest: whakatete, raweke-tia.
Monday: Mane *N.*
money: moni *N.*
month: marama *N.*
monument: koo(w)hatu whakamaharatanga.
moon: marama *N.*
moonlight: atarau *N.*
moor: koraha.
mooring: tauranga *N.*
more: eetahi atu.
morepork: ruru *N*, koukou.
morning: ata *A.*
morning star: Taawera.
morsel: maramara.
mortar: moata *N.*
mortgage: mookete-tia.
mosquito: waeroa *N*, naeroa *N*, naenae *N.*
moss: rimurimu, kohukohu.
moth: puurerehua *N.*
mother: matua wahine, whaea *N*, kookaa *N.*
mother-in-law: hungawai *N*, hungarei *N.*
motion (resolution): mootini.
motor-car: motokaa *N.*
mouldy: waitau *A*, heka.
mound: pukepuke.
mount: eke-a.
mountain: maunga *N.*
mourn: tangi-hia, auee.
mournful: poouri *A.*
mouse: kiore iti.
mouth: maangai *N*, waha *N.*
mouth (of river): ngutu awa, wahapuu *N.*
mouth (side of): paki waha.
move (about): korikori, oreore, nekeneke.

move (aside): kotiti.
move (in some direction): ahu.
move (randomly): hiko.
move (shift): nuku-hia, neke-hia.
mower: moua.
much: nui *A*.
mud, muddy: paru, paruparu *A*.
muesli: muurihi *N*.
mullet: kanae *N*.
multitude: mano, tini *A*, maha *A*.
murder: koohuru-tia.
murmur: koohumuhumu, ngunguru.

muscle: uaua.
mushroom: harore *N*.
musket: puu.
musket (double-barrelled): tuupara.
musket (flintlock): ngutu parera.
mussel: kuku, kuutai.
mussel (freshwater): kaakahi.
muster: taawhiu-a.
mutter: hamumu, nguunguu.
mutton: maatene *N*, miiti hipi.
mutton-bird: tiitii *N*.
my: taaku, tooku, taku, aaku, ooku, aku, waaku.

N

nail *n.*: neera, whao.
naked: noho tahanga, kiri kau, pakiwhara.
name *v.*: hua-ina, tapa-ia.
name *n.*: ingoa.
namely: araa.
narrow: whaaiti *A*.
nation: iwi *N*.
native: tangata maaori, tangata whenua.
navel: pito *N*.
neap tide: tai koowaawaa, tai aa, tai ririki.
near: tata *A*, paatata *A*.
neck: kakii *N*.
neck (back of): ua *N*.
needle: ngira *N*.
nephew: tamaiti, iraamutu *N*.
nest: koo(w)hanga, oowhanga.

net (to make a net): taa kupenga.
net (to net fish): hao-a.
net *n.*: kupenga *N*.
nettle: ongaonga.
neutral: kupapa.
nevertheless: ahakoa.
new: hoou *A*.
news: koorero o te waa, rongo o te waa.
nibble: tiitongi, kakai.
nice: reka *A*, pai *A*.
niece: tamaiti, iraamutu.
night: poo-ngia.
night (last night): inapoo.
nightmare: kuku.
nimble: hohoro *A*, kakama *A*.
nine: iwa *A*.
nineteen: tekau maa iwa.

ninety: iwa tekau.
ninth: tuaiwa.
nip: kikini, kuku-a, pakini.
nipple: koomata.
nit: riha.
no: kaahore, kaao!
nod: tungou.
noise (sound): tangi.
noise (what a noise!): turituri!
  hoihoi!
noon: poupoutanga o te raa,
  awatea.
noose: rore, taawhiti,
  mahanga.
north: raro *L*, hauraro *N*, raki
  N.
north-east wind: paa-
  whakarua.

north wind: hau raro *N*.
nose: ihu *N*.
nostril: pongaihu, pongaponga,
  puta ihu.
not yet: kiaano, kaahore anoo.
notch: teno, tookari-tia.
notwithstanding: he ahakoa.
November: Noema *Pnl.*
novice: tauhoou.
now: aaianei, inaaianei.
nudge: tuke(tuke)-a.
number: nama.
numerous: maha *A*, tini *A*.
nurse *v.* **(a baby):** hiki-tia,
  tapuhi-tia.
nurse *v.* **(a patient):** tapuhi-tia,
  tiaki-na.
nurse *n.*: neehi *N*.

O

oakum: taahunga.
oar: hoe-a.
obedient: ngaawari *A*.
obey: rongo-hia, aata
  whakarongo.
object *v.*: whakakaahore-tia,
  whakahee-ngia.
object *n.*: mea.
oblique: taahapa.
observe: titiro, tiro-hia,
  maatakitaki.
obsidian: mataa tuuhua.
obstacle: aarai-tia, epa,
  tauaarai.
obstinate: turi *A*, tutuu *A*.
obstruct: aarai-tia, taupare-a.

obstructed: kati *P*.
obtain, obtained: whiwhi *A*,
  riro i *P*.
occupation: mahi-a.
occupied: ware-a.
ocean: moana *N*.
ochre, red: kookoowai *N*.
October: Oketopa *Pnl.*
octopus: wheke *N*.
odour: haunga, kakara, piro.
offence: hara *A*, hee *A*.
offensive: weriweri.
offering: whakahere, koha,
  whakaaro.
office: tari *N*.
officer: aapiha *N*.

offspring: uri, whaanau, tamariki.

oil: hinu.

old: tawhito.

old (of people): kaumaatua, koroheke, koroua, kuia.

omen: aituaa, tohu.

ominous: aituaa.

omit: kape-a.

omnipotent: kaha rawa.

one: tahi *A*.

onion: aniana *N*.

only: anake *particle*.

ooze: pipii.

open *a.*: puare *A*, mawhera *P*, tuwhera *A*.

open *v.*: whakapuare-tia, huakina, whakatuwhera-tia.

opening: puta *A*, tomokanga *N*.

opinion: whakaaro.

opossum: paihamu *N*.

oppose: whawhai, aarai-tia, aatete-tia.

opposite: anga-nui, haangai.

opposite side: taawaahi *L*, tarawaahi *L*.

oppress: (taa)taami-a, whakatina-ia.

oracle: matakite, kaupapa.

orange: aarani *N*.

orate: whai-koorero.

oration: whai-koorero.

orator: puu-koorero.

ordain: whakarite-a.

order *n.*, *v.*: tono-a, ngare-a, whakahau-a.

order, put in: whakapai-a, whakatika-ina.

origin: take-a, puutake.

ornament: hei *N*.

ornamental: whakapaipai.

orphan: pani *N*.

oscillate: piupiu-a, ngaaueue.

out: ki waho.

out of breath: heemanawa.

outer: too waho.

outside: waho *L*.

oven: haangi *N*, umu *N*.

over: ki/maa runga.

overawed: hopohopo.

overbearing: haakiki *A*.

overcast: taupuru, kooipuipu, koongu.

overcome: tae (taaea), mate *A*.

overcome (by sleep): parangia (e te moe).

overflow: puurena.

overgrown: ururua.

overhang: tauwhare.

overhanging: areare *A*.

overlap: inaki-tia.

overrun: popoki, pookia.

overthrow, overturn: huri-hia.

overturned: tahuri *P*.

owl: ruru *N*, koukou *N*.

ox: ookiha.

oyster: tio.

P

pack (into): whawhao (whaowhia).

pack *n*.: kawenga *N*, tiikawe.

pack (back): piikau.

pad: whakapuru-a.

paddle: hoe-a.

paddock: paatiki *N*, taiapa.

page (of book): whaarangi.

paid: ea *P*.

pain: mamae.

paint: pani-a, peeita.

pair: puurua, whakapeapea.

palatable: reka *A*.

palate: piki-arero, tako.

pale: maa *A*, koomaa *A*.

paling: waawaa.

palm (of hand): paaroo, kapu.

pan *n*.: peena *N*.

pant: mapu, hotu.

pants: tarau *N*.

paper: pepa *N*.

paradise duck: puutangitangi.

parakeet: kaakaariki.

parch: tunu-a.

pare: waru-hia.

parent: matua *A*.

parrot: kaakaa *N*.

parry: karo-hia.

part: waahi.

participate: uru-a.

partner: hoa.

party (group): ope *N*, roopuu *N*.

party (travelling): tira-(haere) *N*.

pass *n*.: aapiti.

pass away: memeha.

pass behind: nunumi *P*.

pass by: pahure *P*, taha *A*, pahemo *P*.

pass near: konihi.

pass through: puta *A*.

passage: putanga *N*, ara *N*.

passion-fruit: riipeka.

past: paahi.

past (the past): i mua.

pat: pakipaki.

patch: tapi-a, paapaki, pati-a.

path: ara *N*.

patient, be: manawa-nui.

patient, a: tuuroro *N*.

pattern: tauira, ritenga.

pause: okioki, tuu.

pay: utu-a, whakaea-tia.

payment: utu.

pea: pii *N*.

peace: rongo, rangimaarie.

peace (make): hohoutia te rongo.

peach: piititi *N*.

peak: tara, keo, tihi.

peak (of a cap): pare.

peck: timotimo.

pedigree: kaawai.

peel *v*.: waru-hia.

peel *n*.: hiako *N*, kiri *N*, peha *N*.

peep: tirotiro, whakangeingei.

peg: tia-ina.

pelt: epa-ina.

pen: pene *N*.

penalise: whiu-a.

pencil: pene raakau *N*.

penetrate: uru, wero-hia, titi-a.

penguin, little blue: kororaa *N.*
penis: ure *N.*
penny: kapa *N.*
pension: penihana *N.*
people: iwi *N*, taangata.
pepper: pepa *N.*
per cent: paiheneti.
perceive: kite-a.
perch *v.*: tau.
perch *n.*: pae *N.*
perfect: rite tonu, pai rawa atu.
perform: mahi-a.
perhaps: pea *particle.*
perish: mate *A.*
permanent: tuuturu.
permit *v.*: tuku-a.
perpendicular: poupou tonu, tuupoupou.
perplexed: raru *A.*
persevere: tohe-a, kia manawa-nui ki.
person: tangata.
perspiration: werawera, kakawa.
perverse: tutuu.
pervert: whakariro kee, kawe kee.
pestilence: mate urutaa.
pestle: patu, tukituki, paoi.
pet *n.*: mookai.
petrol: penehiini *N*, hinu *N.*
pharmacist: keemihi *N.*
pheasant: peihana *N*, karakata *N.*
phlegm: mare, kea.
photograph *v.*: tango whakaahua.
photograph *n.*: whakaahua.
piano: piana *N.*
pick (cobs of corn): kowhaki-na.
pick (flowers): kato-hia.

pick (gather): kohi-a.
pick (select): whiriwhiri-a, koowhiri-a, koomiri-a.
picnic: pikiniki.
picture: pikitia.
piece: waahi, maramara, piihi.
pied: oopure, purepure.
pierce: wero-hia, poka-ia.
pig: poaka *N.*
pigeon: kereruu *N*, kuukuu *N*, kuukupa *N.*
piles: tero puta.
pillow: urunga, pera *N.*
pilot: kai-urungi, paerata.
pimple: huahua.
pin: pine-a.
pincers: kuku.
pinch: kikini, nonoti, pakini.
pine (black): mataii *N.*
pine (exotic): paina *N.*
pine (red): rimu *N.*
pine (white): kahikatea *N.*
pistol: puu hurihuri, piitara *N.*
pit: rua, koorua, poka.
pity: aroha-ina.
place *n.*: waahi.
place *v.*: waiho-tia, whakanoho-ia.
place (one on another): taapae-a, whakapapa-tia.
plain *n.*: maania *N*, raorao *N*, parae.
plain (clear): maarama.
plait: whiri-a.
plan *v.*: whakatakoto tikanga.
plan *n.*: tikanga *N.*
plane *v.*: kota.
plank: papa.
plant *v.*: whakatoo-kia, ono-kia, tou-a.

plate: pereti N.
platform: atamira N.
play: taakaro-hia, purei-tia.
pleasant: aahuareka, rekareka.
pleased: pai, manawa reka, aahua reka.
Pleiades: Mata-riki.
plentiful: maha A, tini A.
pliable: ngohengohe, ngaawari A.
plough: parau.
ploughshare: hea N.
pluck: whawhaki, kato-hia, ko(w)haki-na.
pluck (a bird): huhuti.
plug: puru-a, kaaremu.
plum: puramu N.
plunder: muru-a.
pocket: paakete N.
point out: tohu-ngia, tuhi-a.
point n.: matamata, tara.
pole: tokotoko.
pole (post): pou.
policeman: pirihimana N.
policy: kaupapa.
polish: whakapiata-tia.
pollen: para.
pool: hoopua N, koopua.
poor: rawakore, poohara.
pop: pakoo.
popcorn: patu wiiti, kaanga paahuuhuu.
porch: roro, whakamahau.
pork: miiti poaka.
porpoise: tuupoupou, upoko-hue N, paapahu N.
porridge: paareti N.
portage: too(a)nga-waka.
porter: kai-amo N.
portion: waahi.

portrait: whakaahua.
position: tuuranga N, takotoranga N.
possess: whiwhi.
possessions: taonga N, taputapu N.
possible: e taaea.
post: pou-a.
post office: poutaapeta N.
pot: koohua, koohue N.
potato: riiwai N, taewa N, parareka N.
pot-bellied: puku wheti, puku teetee.
pound v.: kuru-a, pao-a, tuki-a, patupatu.
pound n.: pauna N.
pour: riringi (ringihia).
pout: (whaka)tupere, tuperu.
powder: paura N.
powder (blasting): paura waawahi.
power: mana A, kaha A.
powerless: kaha kore, miere, ngoikore.
practice (custom): ritenga, tikanga.
practise: parakitihi-tia.
praise: whakapai-a.
pray: inoi-a.
preach: kauwhau-tia.
precipice: pari.
prefect: piriwheke.
pregnant: hapuu.
Premier: Pirimia.
prepare: taka, takatuu.
present n.: koha, whakaaro.
presently: aakuanei.
press v.: peehi, taami-a.
press n.: perehi N.

pretty: aataahua.
prevent: aarai-tia.
price: utu.
prick: wero-hia, oka-ina.
pricked: tuu *P*.
prickly: taratara, koikoi, tiotio.
priest: tohunga.
print: taa-ia, perehi-tia.
printer: kai-taa *N*.
prison: whare-herehere.
private bag: peeke motuhake.
privately: puku *A*.
prize *v*.: kai-ngaakau-tia.
prize *n*.: paraaihe.
proceed: haere.
procreate: ai-tia.
progeny: uri, aitanga *N*.
progress: haere whakamua.
project *v*.: puurero.
project *n*.: kaupapa whakahaere.
promise: oati.
promontory: rae, kuurae, kuumore.
pronounce: whakahua-tia.
proof: tohu, whakaponotanga *N*.
prop up: tautoko-na, tiitoko.
proper: tika *A*.
property: taonga *N*, taputapu *N*.
prophet: poropiti.
propitiate: whakamaarie.
propound: whakatuu.
protect: tiaki-na.
protrude: whererei.
protrude (tongue): whaatero, wheetero.
proud: whakahiihii, whakakake.

prove: whakamaatau-ria.
proverb: whakataukii.
provisional tax: taake taurangi.
provisions: kai, oo *N*.
provoke: whakataritari, whakatenetene, whakatara(tara)-hia.
prow: ihu *N*.
prudent: aata whakaaro.
prune (trim): kokoti (kootia).
psalm: waiata-tia.
public, in: i te aroaro o te katoa.
public house: hooteera *N*, paaparakauta *N*.
publish: paanui-tia, perehi-tia, taa-ia.
pudding: purini *N*.
puff of wind: puurekereke.
pull: kukume (kuumea), too-ia.
pull (against one another): tauwhaatoo.
pull (trigger): keu-a.
pull (up): huhuti, huutia.
pulpy, pulped: peepee *A*, koopeepee.
pulse: mokowhiti *A*.
pulverise: taapaapaa-tia.
pumice: pungapunga.
pumpkin: paukena *N*.
punch *v*.: meke-a.
punch *n*.: panihi.
punch (paper): wero pepa.
punish: whiu-a.
pupil: akonga, tauira *N*.
pupil (of eye): whatu *N*.
puppet: karetao *N*.
purchase: hoko-na mai.
pure: maa *A*.

purify: mea-tia kia maa, whakapai-ngia.
purr: ngeengere.
purse: paahi *N*.
pursue: aru-mia, whai (whaaia).
pus: pirau.

push: pana-a.
put aside: maka-a.
put into: kuhu-a ki.
put (leave): waiho-tia.
put together: huihui-a.
put together (join): tuutui-a.
putrid: pirau.

Q

quack: keekee.
quadruped: kararehe *N*, kurii.
quail: koitareke, wheewhii *N*.
quake: wiri, ngapu, ruu.
qualification (educational): tohu maatauranga.
quantity: nui *A*.
quarrel: pakanga, riri-a, whawhai, totohe.

quarrelsome: tautotohe.
quarter: koata.
queen: kuiini *N*.
quench (fire): tinei-a (ki).
question *n.*: paatai.
question *v.*: paatai-(ngi)a, ui-a.
quick: hohoro, tere, kakama.
quiet: marie *P*, rata, aata noho.
quieted: mauru.
quilt: kuira.

R

rabbit: raapeti *N*.
race (contest): whakataetae-ngia.
race (of people): iwi *N*.
races (horse): purei hooiho.
racquet: raakete *N*.
radio: waerehe *N*, reo irirangi.
raft: mookii, mookihi.
rafter: heke.
rag: karukaru, taretare.
rage, raging: riri-a, nguha.

ragged: kuhakuha, taretare.
rail: rera *N*.
railway: rerewe.
rain: ua-ina, marangai *N*.
rainbow: aaniwaniwa, koopere *N*, Kahukura *Pnl*.
raise, raised: haapai-nga, whakaara-tia, ranga-a, maiangi *P*, rewa *P*.
rake: rakuraku.
ram *v.*: tuki-a

ramrod: tuki-puu.
random: noa *particle*.
range (extent): whaanuitanga.
range (shooting): papa
  puhipuhi.
rank: kapa.
ransom: utu-a.
rap: kuru-a, papaki (paakia).
rapid: tere *A*, au, taaheke.
rape: takahi (wahine).
rascal: rarikena.
rash: hiikaka.
rat: kiore *N*.
rather: engari.
rattle: tatangi.
raw: mata, torouka, ota-ina.
ray: hihi, ihiihi.
razor: heu.
reach: tuupono, tae atu ki,
  tutuki.
reach out: totoro, whaatoro.
read: koorero-tia.
ready: rite *P*, reri *P*.
reap: kokoti (kootia).
rear (child): whaangai-a,
  whakatupu-ria.
rear *n.*: muri *L*.
reason: take-a, tikanga *N*.
recommend: tohutohu.
receipt: riihiiti *N*.
receive: tango-hia (mai).
recent: hoou *A*.
recently: inakua raa.
recite: whakahua-tia, takitaki,
  kauwhau-tia.
recognise: moohio-tia.
recoil: whana.
recollect: mahara-tia.
reconnoitre: toro.
record *n.*: rekoata.

record *v.t.*: tuhi-a.
recriminate: whakawaawaa.
red: whero *A*.
Red Cross: Riipeka Whero.
red hot: kakaa.
red ochre: kookoowai, horu.
reddish: puuwhero,
  wherowhero.
redeem: hoko-na.
reduce (size or number):
  whakaiti-a, whakaheke-a.
reduce (by paring down,
  squeezing in): runa-a.
redundancy pay: utu
  whakamutu mahi.
reed: kaakaho *N*.
referee: rewherii-tia.
reflect: whakaata.
reflected image: ata.
refractory: hianga, tutuu.
refresh: whakangaa,
  whakahauora.
refreshment: ora *A*.
refuge: piringa.
refuse: whakakaahore-tia,
  whakaparahako-tia.
region: waa, takiwaa *N*.
regret, regretful: aroha,
  koonohi.
reins: reina, taura *N*.
reject: whakarere-a,
  whakaparahako.
rejoice: hari, koa *A*.
relation: whanaunga *N*,
  huaanga.
relaxing, relaxed: paarore.
release: tuku-a.
relieve: riiwhi.
reliever: kai-riiwhi.
religion: haahi *N*.

relish *n.*: kiinaki *N.*
repulsive: wetiweti, weriweri, moorikarika.
report *n.*: puurongo(rongo), taapaetanga *N*, riipoata *N*, koorero tuku.
request: inoi-a.
requite, be requited: whakaea, ea *P.*
resemblance: ritenga *N.*
resemble: rite *A.*
reserve: raahui-tia, taapui-tia.
reserve (substitute): kai-riiwhi.
residence: kaainga *N*, whare *N.*
resin: kaapia *N.*
resist: whawhai, riri-a, aatete.
resolute: maaroo, uaua, maaia *A.*
resound: pakuu, paoro, haruru.
respire: whakaea, ngaa.
rest: okioki.
restaurant: wharekai *N.*
restless: taahurihuri, okeoke.
restrain: (pu)puri-tia.
result: tukunga iho, hua.
retch: puutanetane, ruaki-na.
retire (cease work): whakangaa.
return *v.i.*: hoki-a.
return *v.t.*: whakahoki-a.
reveal: whakakite-a, whakapuaki-na, whaaki-na.
revenge, avenged: utu-a, ea *P*, ngaki-a.
reverberate: haruru, paoro.
revile: taunu.
revive: whakahauora.
reward: utu.
rheumatism: ruumaatiki.
rib: kaokao, rara.
ribbon: riipene *N.*

rice: raihi *N.*
rich: whai taonga.
riddle: kai, panga.
ride: eke (hoiho).
rider: kai-eke.
ridge: hiwi, pae maunga.
ridgepole: taahuhu.
rifle: raiwhara.
right (authority): mana *A.*
right (correct): tika *A*, tootika *A.*
right hand: ringa matau.
rim: ngutu, tapa.
rind: hiako, peha.
ring *n.*: riingi *N.*
rip: paawhara-tia, tiihore.
ripe: maoa.
ripple: kare.
rise up: ara, maranga, whakatika.
river: awa *N.*
road: huanui, huarahi, ara, roori.
roam: haaereere, taka, kootiititi.
roast: tunu-a.
rob: paahua-tia, taahae-tia, whaanako-tia.
robin: piitoitoi *N.*
rock: koowhatu, poowhatu, toka, kaamaka.
roe: hua, pewa, pee.
roll: hurihuri, porotiti.
roller: neke, rango.
Rome: Rooma *L.*
roof: tuanui.
room: ruuma *N.*
root *v.*: ketu-a.
root *n.*: pakiaka, paiaka.
rope: taura *N*, kaha, ropi.

rope ladder: ara taura.
rotten: pirau.
rough: taratara.
rough (of the sea): ngarungaru, karekare.
round: porotaka, poro(w)hita.
round about: aawhio, taiawhio.
rouse: whakaoho.
row (line): raarangi, kapa.
royalty (on asset): paru *N*.
rub: miri-a.
rubber: rapa *N*.
rubbish: otaota, parapara, raapihi.
rubbish-tin: tini raapihi.
rudder: urungi.
rule: tikanga *N*.
ruler (measure): ruuri *N*.
rumble: haruru, ngunguru.
run: oma-kia.
runner (of a plant): kaawai, torotoro.
rupture (hernia): whaturama.
rush: huaki-na.
Russia: Ruuhia *L*.
rust: waikura.
rustle: ngaehe.

S

sabbath: hapati *N*.
sack: peeke *N*.
sacrament: hakarameta *N*.
sacred: tapu *A*.
sacrifice: patunga tapu.
sad: poouri.
saddle: tera *N*, nohoanga.
saddleback: tieke *N*.
saddlecloth: whakapuru tera, whaariki.
safe: ora *A*.
safeguard: maru *A*.
safety: ora *A*, oranga *N*.
sail *v.*: rere.
sail *n.*: raa *N*, heera *N*.
sailor: heramana *N*.
saint: tangata tapu.
sale: hoko-na, hokohoko.
saliva: huu(w)are, haaware.
salt: tote *N*.
salvation: oranga *N*.
same: oorite, taurite.
Samoa: Haamoa *L*.
sanctify: whakatapu.
sand: onepuu *N*.
sandbank: taahuna *N*.
sandfly: namu *N*.
sanitary pad: kope wahine.
sap: pia *N*.
sapling: maahuri, koohuri.
sapwood: taitea *N*.
satisfied: maakona *P*, naa, ngata.
satisfy: whakanaa.
Saturday: Haatarei *N*.
saucepan: hoopane *N*.
saucer: hoeha, hoohi.
save: whakaora, tohu-ngia.
saviour: kaiwhakaora.
savour: kakara, rongo.

saw: kani.
saw (hacksaw): kani maitai.
saw (machine saw): kani
   miihini.
say: koorero-tia, kii-a, mea-tia.
saying: whakataukii, kupu *N*,
   koorero-tia.
scab: paku.
scale (of fish): unahi *N*.
scar *n*.: riwha *A*, nawe.
scare: whakawehi,
   whakamataku-ria.
scarifier (implement):
   karawhaea.
scatter: rui-a, whakakorakora.
scattered: marara *P*, tiirara,
   tihehu.
scent: kakara, tiare *N*.
schism: wehewehenga *N*.
scholar: aakonga *N*, tauira.
scholarship: karahipi.
school: kura, whare-kura.
scissors: kuti(kuti).
scold: ko(w)hete-tia.
scoop: tiikaro-tia, koko-a.
scorch: hunuhunu, hana.
score (tally): tatau-ria.
Scotch thistle: kootimana,
   katimana.
scour: horoi-a.
scout: tuutei *N*, tuutai *N*,
   torotoro.
scrap: toenga *N*, maramara.
scrape: waru-hia, haaroo,
   wania.
scratch: ra(ku)raku, rarapi.
scream: kowee, tiwee, auee,
   tangi-hia, ngawii.
screen: aarai-a.
scribe: kai-tuhituhi *N*.

scrofula: mate pokapoka.
scrub: horoi-a.
scull: kooue, ue.
scythe: hai.
sea: moana, tai.
sea breeze: muri-tai, hau
   moana.
sea urchin: kina *N*.
sea-coast: tahatai *N*, taatahi *L*,
   aakau *N*, takutai *N*, taha
   moana.
seal: kekeno *N*.
seal (stamp): hiiri-tia.
seam: tuinga *N*.
search: rapu-a, haahaa,
   kimi-hia.
season: tau, waa.
seat: nohoanga *N*, tuuru *N*.
seaweed: rimurimu.
second (in order): tuarua.
second (of time): heekena.
secret *a*.: puku.
secretary.: hekeretari *N*.
section: waahanga *N*.
sediment: para.
see: kite-a.
seed: purapura, koopura,
   kaakano.
seek: rapu-a, kimi-hia, haahaa,
   haahau-tia.
seer: mata-kite.
seesaw: tiemi.
segment: tapahanga *N*.
seize: hopu-kia, kapo-hia.
seized: mau *P*.
select: whiriwhiri-a,
   koowhiri-a.
select (sort out): koomiri-a.
selfish: moohuu.
sell: hoko-na.

send: tono-a, ngare-a, unga-a, tuku-a.

separate *a*.: motuhake.

separate *v*.: (wehe)wehe-a, wawae-a, motu-hia, mawehe *P*, tauwehe *P*.

separator: haapareta.

September: Hepetema *Pnl*.

sermon: kauwhau-tia.

serpent: naakahi, ngaakahi.

servant: kaimahi *N*, pononga *N*.

serve, be served (of food): rato *P*, whakarato-hia.

service: (roopuu) aawhina.

set (a net): whakapaa kupenga.

set (a sail): kookiri-tia.

set (in place): whakanoho-ia.

set (of sun): too, torengi.

set up: whakatuu-ria, -hia.

settle (as a bird): tau.

settle (as people): noho.

settle(d) (as a matter): tatuu, tau.

seven: whitu *A*.

seventeen: tekau maa whitu.

seventh: tuawhitu.

seventy: whitu tekau.

sever: (mo)motu-hia, wawae-a.

sew: tuitui.

sex (gender): taane, wahine.

shade: whakamarumaru, marumaru.

shadow: ata *N*.

shag (black): kawau *N*, koau *N*.

shake: ngaaueue, oioi, rurerure, ngarue, ruu(ruu).

shake hands: ruuruu, (w)hariruu.

shallow: paapaku.

shame: whakamaa.

shape: aahua *N*.

share: hea, waahi.

shark: mangoo *N*.

sharp: koi *A*.

sharpen: whakakoi-a.

shave: heu-a.

she: ia *Pnl*.

shear: kutikuti.

shears: kutikuti.

sheath: puukoro.

shed: wharau.

sheep: hipi *N*.

sheet: hiiti *N*.

shell: anga, kota.

shellfish (bivalve): pipi, kuku.

shellfish (univalve): puupuu.

shelter: taawharau-tia, whakamarumaru.

sheltered (from rain, wind): ruru.

sheltered (from sun): marumaru.

shepherd: heepara *N*.

shield: puapua, hiira.

shilling: herengi *N*.

shin: taataa.

shine, shining: tiaho, whiti-a, piiataata *A*.

ship: kaipuke *N*.

shirt: haate *N*.

shiver: wiri, huukiki.

shoal (of fish): tere, rara, ranga.

shoal (sandbank): taahuna *N*.

shoe: huu.

shoot: wene, torotoro, tupu, pihipihi.

shoot (of gun): pupuhi (puuhia).

shore: takutai *L*, tahatai,
   tahaki *L*, uta *L*, tai *L*.
short: (po)poto, hakahaka.
shorten: whakapoto-hia.
shorts: tarau poto.
shoulder *v.*: amo-hia,
   paakawe-tia.
shoulder *n.*: pakihiwi,
   pokohiwi.
shout: karanga-tia, pararee,
   umere-tia, tiiwaha,
   haamama.
shove: tute-a.
shovel: haapara *N*, haawera,
   tiikoko-a.
show: whakakite-a,
   whakaatu-ria.
shower: ua-ina.
shred: hukahuka.
shrill: tiioro.
shrivelled: memenge,
   (ngi)ngio.
shudder: wi(ni)wini *A*.
shut, be shut: kati *A*, kopani-a,
   paa-ia.
shy *a.*: (hi)hira.
shy *v.*: oho.
sick: mate *A*, maauiui.
sickle: toronaihi *N*.
sickness: mate *A*,
   maauiuitanga.
side: taha *A*, kaokao *N*.
side (other): tua *L*, taawaahi *L*.
side (to one): tahaki *L*.
sideways: kootaha, tiitaha.
sieve: taatari-tia, hiitari.
sift: taatari-tia, hiitari.
sigh: mapu.
sight *v.*: kite-a.
sight *n.*: kitenga *N*.

sight (almost out of):
   moonenehu.
sight (out of): nunumi *P*.
sign: tohu-ria.
signal: tohu-ria.
silent: noho-puku, haanguu.
sill: pehipehi.
silly: heahea, huke, rorirori.
silt: kenepuru.
silver: hiriwa *N*.
silver-eye: tauhou *N*, karu-
   paatene *N*, pihipihi.
similar: rite.
simile: kupu whakarite.
simplify (explain):
   whakamaarama-tia.
simplify (make easier):
   whakamaamaa-tia.
simulate (make like):
   whakarite-a.
sin: hara *A*.
since (because): ina *particle*, i te
   mea, ina hoki.
since (the time): mai (anoo).
sinew: uaua.
sing: waiata-tia.
singe: hunuhunu-a.
single: tapatahi.
singlet: hingareti *N*.
singly: takitahi.
sink: totohu *P*.
sinker: maahee, maihea.
sinner: tangata hara.
sir (term of address): koro,
   paa.
Sir (title): Taa.
Sirius: Takurua.
sister (of female): teina,
   tuakana.
sister (of male): tuahine.

sister-in-law: taokete, auwahine.
sit: noho-ia.
sit (on heels): noho tiineinei.
site: papanga, paenga, tuunga.
six: ono.
sixpence: hikipene *N*.
sixteen: tekau maa ono.
sixth: tuaono.
sixty: ono tekau.
size: nui *A*, rahi *A*.
skeleton: kooiwi *N*.
skill: moohio-tia, maatau-ria,
tohungatanga *N*, rawe *A*.
skilled: moohio-tia, rawe *A*.
skim (along surface): tipi.
skin: kiri *N*, hiako *N*, tapeha
N, peha *N*.
skip: mawhiti.
skulk: piri.
skull: angaanga.
sky: rangi *N*.
sky-lark: manu kakahi.
slab: papa.
slack: korokoro,
haangorongoro.
slacken: whakakorokoro,
tukutuku-a.
slant: konana.
slap: papaki (paakia).
slasher: (pere)huuka.
slaughter: patu-a.
slave: taurekareka.
sledge: kooneke, paanuku.
sleep: moe-a.
sleepy: hiamoe, momoe.
sleepyhead: moeroa.
slide: mania-a.
slime: ware.
sling: kootaha *N*, piu-a.

slink: ninihi.
slip: mania, parengo.
slip (of a knot): hangoro.
slippery: mania, paaremoremo,
paarengorengo.
slit: hahae.
slope (gentle): paananaki.
slope (steep): harapaki.
slothful: maangere *A*.
slow: roa *A*, whakaroa-tia,
pooturi *A*.
sludge: paruparu.
slug: ngata.
smack the lips: kootamutamu.
small: iti *A*, nohinohi *A*,
pakupaku *A*.
smart: kakama *A*.
smash: taiari-tia, pao-a,
tiitari-tia.
smash, smashed: pakaru *P*,
taiari-tia, pao-a.
smear: pani-a.
smell: hongi-a, rongo-hia.
smile: menemene nga
paapaaringa, menemene ki te
kata.
smoke: paoa, auahi.
smoke (tobacco): kai
paipa.
smooth *a*.: maaeneene *A*.
smooth *v*.: whakaene.
smoulder: mohu.
snag *n*.: taitaa.
snagged: mau *P*.
snail: ngata.
snake: naakahi *N*, neke *N*.
snap: motu *P*, momotu,
mootuhia, whati *P*,
whawhati, whaatiia.
snapper: taamure *N*.

snare: rore-a, taawhiti *N*, mahanga-tia.
snatch: kapo-hia, hopu-kia.
sneak: haere toropuku.
sneer: taawai-a.
sneeze: tihe, matihe, tihao.
sniff: hongihongi.
snore: ngongoro.
snort: whengu.
snout: ihu *N*.
snow: huka, huka-rere.
soak: tuku ki te wai, koopirotia.
soap: hopi *N*.
soar: whakatopa.
sob: hotu *A*.
sock: tookena *N*.
socket: koo(w)hao *N*.
soft: ngaawari *A*, ngohengohe *A*.
soften: whakangaawari-tia.
softly: maarire.
soil: oneone *N*.
soiled: paru *A*.
solder: piuta *N*.
soldier: hooia *N*.
sole (fish): paatiki rori.
sole (of foot): kapukapu, takahanga *N*.
solid: maaroo, pakeke.
solitary: mokemoke *A*.
son: tamaiti taane.
son-in-law: hunaonga.
song: waiata-tia, tau.
soon: meake, aaianei, tata anoo.
soot: awe.
soothe: whakamaarie.
sore, *a.*: mamae.
sorrow, sorrowful: poouri *A*.

sort: tuu, aahua *N*.
soul: wairua *N*.
sound: tangi-hia.
sound (depth of water): taaweewee.
sound (of sleep): au te moe.
sour: kawa *A*.
source: maataapuna, pukenga, puu, take.
south: tonga *N*, runga *L*.
south-east: puutongatonga-marangai.
south-west: tonga maauru.
sow (pig): uwha poaka.
sow (seed): rui-a.
sow-thistle: puuhaa.
space (interval): tiriwa-tia.
spade: kaaheru *N*, koo-ia, hoo, pei *N*.
spade (in cards): peeti *N*.
Spaniard: Paaniora *N*.
spanner: taanakuru.
spare *v.*: tohu-ngia.
spark: korakora ahi.
sparrowhawk: kaarearea.
speak: kii-a, mea-tia, koorerotia.
spear *v.*: wero-hia.
spear *n.*: tao *N*, matarau *N*, kookiri.
special (separate): motuhake.
speck: kora, tongi.
speckled: tongitongi, kootingotingo.
spectacles: moowhiti.
speech: koorero-tia, kii-a, kupu *N*, reo *N*.
speech (formal oration): whaikoorero.
speed: hohoro, tere *A*.

spell (charm): karakia.

spell (words): tatau (tau-ria).

spent: pau *P*, hemo *P*.

sperm-whale: paraaoa.

spider: puungaawerewere.

spike: taratara.

spill: ringi-hia.

spilt: maringi *P*.

spin (of thread): miro-a.

spine (backbone): iwi tuararo.

spine (of fish, sea urchins, etc.): tara.

spirit: wairua.

spit: tuwha-ina.

spittle: huare *N*, haaware.

splash, splashed: poorutu, poohutuhutu, whekuwheku.

splice: hono-a.

splinter: maramara.

split: waawahi, waahia.

spoil: whakakino-tia, takakino.

spongy: puukahukahu.

spoon: pune *N*, puunu *N*.

sport: taakaro.

spot: tongi, tiwha.

spotted: kootiwhatiwha.

spouse: hoa, tahu.

spout *n.*: koorere.

sprained: takoki *P*.

sprat: aua *N*.

spray: rehutai.

spread: whaariki-tia, mahora *P*.

spring *v.*: whana, tuurapa.

spring (of water): puna.

spring tide: tai nunui.

sprinkle: uwhiuwhi-a.

sprout: pihi, tupu-ria.

spur: kipa, kiki.

spurt: hiirere, patii.

spy: tuutai, tuutei.

square (four sided): tapawhaa.

square (tool): koea.

squeak: kotokoto, tiitii.

squeal: auee, ngawii.

squeeze: roromi.

squid: wheke *N*, nguu *N*.

squint: keko, rewha.

stab: oka-ina, wero-hia.

stable: teepara *N*.

stack: whakapuu, taapae-a, taake-tia.

staff: tokotoko-na.

stage: pourewa, atamira *N*, whata.

stagger: turori, hiirori.

stained: poke *P*.

stairs: arawhata.

stake: poupou.

stalk: kakau *N*.

stallion: taariana *N*.

stand: tuu.

staple *n.*: teepara *N*.

star: whetuu *N*.

stare: titiro puu.

stare wildly: whetee.

start (begin): tiimata-ria.

start (sudden movement): oho, taakiri-tia.

startle: whakaoho-kia.

starve *v.i.*: mate i te kai.

station: teihana *N*, tuuranga *N*.

statue: whakapakoko.

stay: noho-ia.

steal: taahae-tia, whaanakotia.

stealthily go: ninihi, haere kuhu.

steam: korohuu *N*, puia.

steamer: tima *N*.

steamy: puumaahu.

steep: poupoua, tuuparipari.
steer: urungi-tia, tia-ina.
stench: piro, haunga.
step: hiikoi.
step (of ladder): kaupae, pae.
stern (of boat): kei.
sternpost: taurapa *N*.
Stewart Island: Rangi-ura *L*.
stick *n*.: raakau.
stick (stab): oka-ina, wero-hia.
stick, be stuck (adhere): rapa *A*, whakarapa-ngia.
stiff: maaroo, pakeke.
still (of water): marino *A*.
still (stand still): tuu maarika.
still *ad*.: anoo *particle*, tonu *particle*.
stilt (pied): toorea.
stilts: waewae raakau.
sting: wero-hia, kakati.
sting-ray: whai *N*, paakaurua.
stingy: kaiponu-hia, haakere-a.
stink: piro *A*, haunga *A*.
stir: koorori-a.
stirrup: terapu, tarapu.
stitch: tuitui-a.
stockade: paa-tuuwatawata.
stocking: tookena *N*.
stomach: puku.
stone: koowhatu *N*, poowhatu *N*.
stool: tuuru *N*.
stoop: piko, koropiko, tuuohu.
stop (block up, plug): puru-a.
stop (halt): tuu *A*.
stop (prevent): aarai-tia.
stop (restrain, hold back): pupuri, puri-tia.
stopped (blocked): puni, paa *A*.
store (shop): toa *N*.

storehouse: paataka *N*, whata, paakoro.
storm: tupuhi, aawhaa.
stouthearted: manawa-nui.
stove: too *N*.
straight: tootika *A*, tika *A*.
straighten: whakatika-ia.
strain (by sieve, or wringing): taatari-tia.
strain (stretch tight): whakamaarooroo-tia.
strainer (sieve): taatari.
strand of rope: kanoi.
stranger: tauhoou *N*.
strangle: nonoti, nootia, taarona.
strap: tarapu *N*.
straw: taakakau.
street: huarahi, huanui, tiriti.
strength: kaha *A*.
strenuous: uaua.
stretch: whakamaaro, kukume (kuumea).
stretch (out): totoro, torona.
stride: hiikoi.
strike: patu-a, tuki-a, moto-kia, pao-a.
string: tau, miro, tiringi, tuaina.
strip: muru-a, tiihore-a.
strive: whakauaua, tohe-a.
stroke: hokomirimiri.
stroll: haaereere.
strong: kaha, pakari, maarooroo.
struck: paa, whara *P*, tuu *P*.
struggle: oke-a.
stubborn: pouturi.
stuff up: puru-a.
stumble: tuutuki.

stump: tumu, take.

stunted: puukiki.

sty: raaihe poaka.

stye: kiritona.

subject: take.

subside: heke *A*, whakamauru.

subtract: tango-hia.

succeed (replace): whakakapi.

successor: kai-riiwhi *N*, mimiti *A*.

succour: awhina-tia.

suck: ngote-a, momi-a.

suddenly: whakarere.

suffer: mate *A*, mamae.

suffocate: nonoti, nootia.

sugar: huka *N*.

suit (of clothes): huutu *N*, huiti *N*.

suitable: tau, rawe.

sulk: whererei.

sulphur: whanariki.

summarise: whakaraapopoto-ngia.

summer: raumati.

summit: tihi.

summons: haamene-tia.

sun: raa *N*.

sunbeam: hihi o te raa.

sunburnt: manauri i te raa.

Sunday: Raa-tapu *N*.

sunrise: te putanga o te raa.

supper: hapa.

supple: ngohengohe, ngaawari, ngorengore.

supplement: taapiri-tia, turuki.

support: whakawhirinaki-tia, tautoko-na.

suppose: whakaaro-tia.

suppress: peehi-a, taawhi-a, taami-a.

sure: moohio-tia.

surf: karekare.

surfeited: maakona *P*, ngaaruru, whiu *P*.

surly: pukuriri.

surpass: hipa.

surprise (ambush): komutu-a, hopu-kia.

surprised: miiharo.

surrender: tuku-a.

surround: karapoti-a, pae-a.

survey: ruuri-tia.

survivor: moorehu.

suspect: whakapae-ngia.

suspend, suspended: whakairi-a, iri *A*, mooiri.

suspicious, suspicion: tuupato, moohio.

swagger: whakataamaramara.

swallow: horomi-a.

swamp: repo.

swamp hen: puukeko *N*, paakura *N*.

swan: kaawana *N*.

swarm: mui-a.

sweat: kakawa, werawera.

sweep: tahi-a, puruma-tia.

sweet: reka *A*.

sweetheart: whaiaaipo, tau, ipo.

swell: puku, pupuhi.

swift: hohoro, tere, kakama *A*.

swim: (kau) kau-ria, kauhoe-tia, kautaahoe.

swing *v.*: taarere.

swing *n.*: moorere *N*.

switch: keu-a.

sword: hoari.

symptom: tohu.

synod: hiinota *N*.

T

table: teepu N.
tablecloth: uhi teepu.
tack (of ship): waihape.
tail (of animal): whiiore N, teera.
tail (of bird): remu, kootore N.
tail (of fish): hiku N.
take: tango-hia.
take off (of clothes): unu-hia, tango-hia.
talk: koorero-tia.
tall: roa A, teitei.
tame: rata A.
tamper with: raweke-tia, hiianga-tia.
tap: koorere N.
tap-dance: tepetepe.
tape (audio): riipene N.
tapered: kaawitiwiti.
tap-root: more.
tarpaulin: taapoorena.
taste v.: rongo-hia.
taste n.: rongo, haa.
tattoo v.: taa-ia.
tattoo n.: moko N.
taunt: taawai-a, taunu.
tax n.: taake N.
taxi: taakihi N.
tea: tii N.
tea (tea-leaves): tiitii-rau.
teach: ako-na, whakaako-na.
teacher: maahita N, kai-whakaako N.
team: tiima N.
teapot: tiipaata.
tear: tiitore-a, ngahae A.
tear (in weeping): roimata N.

tease: taawai-a, whakatoi, whakatara-ngia.
teat: uu N, titi N.
tea-tree: maanuka N, kahikaatoa N.
telegram: waea-tia.
telephone: whounu N, riingi-tia, waea-tia.
television: pouaka whakaata, tiiwii.
tell: whakaatu-ria, whaaki-na, koorero-tia, mea-tia.
teller (bank): kai-tatau moni.
temperature: mahana.
temple: temepara N.
tempt: whakamaatautau-ria.
ten: tekau A.
tender: ngaawari A, ngohengohe A.
tendon: uaua.
tennis: tenehi, tenihi.
tent: teneti N.
termination: mutunga N.
tern: tara N.
terrible: wehi A, mataku A.
terrify: whakamataku-ria, whakawehi-a.
testament: kaawenata N.
testicle: raho N.
testify: whakaatu-ria.
thank: whakapai-a, whakawheetai, mihi, whakamihi.
thank you!: ka pai! e tika raa hoki!
thatch: ato-hia, taapatu-tia.

thereby: na/no reira, na konei, maa reira.

therefore: na/no reira, koia.

these: eenei.

they: raaua, raatou *Pnl.*

thick: maatotoru *A.*

thicket: taaeo.

thief: taahae-tia, kaiaa *N*, whaanako-tia.

thigh: kuu(w)haa, huu(w)haa *N.*

thin: rahirahi *A*, angiangi *A.*

thin (lean): tuupuhi, (w)hiiroki, tuu(w)ai.

thing: mea.

think: whakaaro-tia, maharatia, mea-tia.

third: tuatoru, toru.

thirst, thirsty: mate-wai, hiainu.

thirteen: tekau maa toru.

thirty: toru tekau.

this: teenei.

thistle (sow): puu(w)haa.

thistle (Scotch thistle): kootimana, poonitanita.

thorn: koikoi.

thoroughly: aata, maarire *P.*

thought: mahara-tia, whakaaro-tia.

thousand: mano *A.*

thread *v.*: tui-a.

thread *n.*: miro, tarete.

thread-worm: iroiro.

threaten: whakawehi-a.

three: toru *A.*

thresh: whiu-a.

threshold: paepae.

throat: korokoro *N.*

throb: kapakapa, panapana.

throne: toroona *N.*

throng *v.*, *n.*: taamuimui-a, huihui-a.

throughout: puta noa.

throw: maka-a, panga-ia, whiu-a.

thrum: hukahuka.

thrush: piopio.

thrust: kookiri-tia.

thud: takuru.

thumb: koromatua, koonui.

thump: taakurukuru, kuru-a.

thunder: whatitiri, whaitiri.

Thursday: Taaite *N.*

thus: peenei.

thwart *n.*: taumanu.

ticket: tiiketi *N.*

tickle *v.*: (whaka)ngaoko.

tickle *n.*: rekareka, ngaoko.

tide: tai.

tide (ebb): tai timu.

tide (flood): tai pari.

tidings: rongo.

tie: here-a, whiitiki-tia, pona-ia.

tie (necktie): neketai *N.*

tiger: taika *N.*

tight: mau *P*, kita, kikii.

tighten: whakakikii-tia.

till (until): tae noa ki, taaea noatia.

tilt: whakatiitaha.

timber: raakau *N.*

time: waa, taaima *N.*

timid: wehi *A*, mataku *A.*

tinder: puu tawa.

tingle: tiioro, wheeoro.

tip: matamata, koinga *N.*

tired: ngenge *A*, maauiui, hoohaa *A.*

tiresome: poorearea.
toast (heat): tunu-a.
toast (propose a): toohi-tia.
tobacco: tupeka, torori, paipa.
today: (n)aaianei *L*.
toe: matimati, matikara.
toe (big): koonui, koromatua.
toe (little): koroiti, tooiti.
together: tahi, ngaatahi.
toil: mamahi, whakauaua, mahi-a.
tomb: urupaa.
tomorrow: aapoopoo *L*.
ton: tana *N*.
tongs: piinohi-tia.
tongue: arero *N*.
too: hoki *particle*, anoo *particle*.
tooth: niho *N*.
toothache: niho tunga.
toothbrush: paraahi niho.
top, spinning: pootaka, kaihootaka, kaihoorapa.
top, the: runga *L*.
topknot: koukou, tikitiki.
torch: rama.
torment: whakamamae-tia.
torn: pakaru *P*, ngahae.
toss: piu-a, whiu-a.
total: te katoa, te nui.
touch: paa-ngia, whakapaa.
tough: uaua, maaroo.
tourist: tuuruhi *N*.
tow *v.*: tootoo, kukume (kuumea).
towel: tauera *N*, taawera *N*, taaora *N*.
town: taaone *N*.
track *n.*: ara, huarahi.

tractor: tarakihana *N*, tarakitaa *N*.
trade: hoko-na, hokohoko-na.
tradition: koorero tupuna, hiitori *N*.
train (railway): tereina.
tramp, trample: takahi-a.
transgress: ngau kee.
translate: whakamaaori-tia.
transparent: maarama kehokeho.
trap: rore-a, taawhiti *N*.
travel: haere-a, takihaere.
tread: takahi-a.
treasure: taonga *N*.
treaty: tiriti *N*.
tree: raakau *N*.
tremble: wiri.
trevally: araara.
trial: whakamaatauranga *N*.
tribe: hapuu, iwi.
tribunal: taraipiunara *N*.
trickle: maaturuturu.
trigger: keu *N*.
trip up: hiirau-tia.
troop *n.*: ope, maatua.
tropic-bird: amokura *N*.
trot (of horse): toitoi, taawai.
trouble: aituaa *A*, raruraru.
troublesome: whangawhanga, haututuu.
trough: kumete *N*, oko.
trousers: tarau.
truck: taraka.
true: pono.
trump: taanapu-tia.
trumpet: puu-taatara, teetere.
trunk (of tree): tinana *N*.
trust: whakapono.
truth: pono *A*.

try: whakamaatau-ria.
tub: taapu *N*.
Tuesday: Tuurei *N*.
tuft: purepure, puhipuhi.
tumble: hinga *P*, taka *A*.
tumour: puku.
tune: rangi *N*.
turkey: korukoru, piipipi.
turn: huri-hia, tahuri *P*.
turn (aside): hipa, peka.
turn (back): hoki-a.
turn (from side to side): whakatahataha.
turn (inside out): huri kooaro.
turn (over and over): tiitakataka.
turn (revolve): porotiti.

turn (the back): huri kootua.
turn (upside down): huri taupoki.
turnip: keha, koorau.
tusk: rei, niho puta.
tweezers: kuku-a.
twelve: tekau maa rua.
twenty: rua tekau.
twice: tuarua.
twinkle: rikoriko.
twins: maahanga *N*.
twirl: porotiti.
twist: whiri-a, miro-a, kaawiri-tia, takawiri-tia.
twisted (of timber): takawiri, koorori.
twitch: taakiri-tia.
two: rua *A*.

U

ugly: aahua kino.
ulcerated: koomaoa.
umbilical cord: iho.
umbrella: amarara, marara.
unaware: ware-a, kuu(w)are *A*.
uncertain: rangirua.
uncle: matua keekee.
uncooked: mata *A*, kaimata, ota *A*.
uncover, uncovered: hura-hia, huke-a, mahura *P*.
uncultivated (of land): papatua.
undecided: whakaangaanga, wheeangaanga, aawangawanga.
under: i/kei raro.

understand: maatau-ria (ki), moohio-tia (ki), kite-a.
undone: matara *P*.
uneven (of a surface): paahiwihiwi.
unfledged bird: koorahoraho.
unfortunate: aituaa.
unfruitful: hua-kore, tuupaa, taataa-kau.
unintelligible: kaahore i te maarama.
unite: whakakotahi.
unity: kotahitanga *N*.
unjust: hee *A*.
unless: ki te kore.
unlucky: aituaa.

unmindful: wareware.
unoccupied: waatea *P*.
unpaid: taarewa.
unpalatable: kawa *A*.
unravel: (wete)wete-kia,
whakamatara.
unripe: mata, kaimata,
ota.
unseasoned (of timber):
kaimata.
unsteady: tiitaka, tatutatu,
hiirori *A*.
untie, untied: (wete)wete-kia,
mawete, matara.

until: tae noa ki, taaea noatia.
untouched: urutapu.
unyielding: whakatuturi.
upon: i runga.
uppermost: too runga rawa.
upright: tuu tonu, tuu tika.
upset: tahuri *P*.
urge: akiaki-na, ngare-a.
urine: mimi.
us: taaua, maaua, taatou,
maatou.
use: tangotango.
utter: whakapuakina.
uvula: tohetohe.

V

vacant: waatea, takoto noa.
vagina: ara tamariki.
valley: awaawa, riu, whaarua.
value: utu, waariu, ritenga *N*.
vanity: whakahiihii.
vapour: mamaoa.
variable: haurokuroku.
vary: puta kee, tiitaha.
veal: (miiti) kuuao piiwhi.
veil: koopare, aarai-tia.
vein: uaua.
venereal disease: paipai,
pakiwhara, mate kino.
veranda(h): (whaka)mahau,
parana.
verse (stanza): whiti.
very: tino *N*, rawa *particle*.
vex, vexed: raru *A*, rangirangi-
a, whanowhano-a.
vibrate: ngatari, ruu, wiriwiri.
victorious: toa *A*.

victory: wikitooria *N*.
view: tirohanga.
vigilant: mataara.
vile: weriweri, whakarihariha.
village: kaainga *N*.
vine: waina *N*.
violate: takahi.
violent: taikaha.
virgin: waahina, puhi.
viscid: tatakii.
vise: kuku.
vision: kitenga *N*, matakite.
visit: toro, whakatau-a.
visitor: manuhiri.
voice: reo *N*.
volley: taipara.
vomit: ruaki-na.
vote: pooti-tia.
vow: oati-tia.
vowel (letter): reta puare.
vowel (sound): oro puare.

W

wag: tooroherohe.
wages: utu.
waggon: waakena N.
wail: auee, tangi-hia.
waist: hope N.
wait: tatari, taaria, whanga.
wake v.i.: ara, oho.
wake v.t.: whakaara-hia,
   whakaoho-kia.
walk: haere-a-waewae, haere
   ma raro.
walking-stick: tokotoko.
wall: pakitara, paatuu.
wallet: paahi.
wander: haereere, kootiti haere.
wanderer: manene.
want: hiahia-tia, piirangi-tia.
war: pakanga-tia, whawhai.
ward off: papare, aarai-tia,
   kakaro.
warm a.: mahana A, werawera
   A.
warm v.: whakawerawera.
warn: whakatuupato-ria.
warrior: toa A.
wart: tona N, kiritona N.
wary: matakana, tuupato.
was: See under be.
wash: horoi-a.
wasp: waapu, waapi.
waste: moumou.
watch v.: mataki.
watch n.: wati N.
water: wai.
water (fresh): wai maaori.
water (salt): wai tai.
water-cress: waata-kirihi.

waterfall: rere, taaheke.
wave v.: poowhiri-tia.
wave n.: ngaru N.
way: ara N.
we: taaua, maaua, taatou,
   maatou.
weak: ngoikore A.
weak (of will): hauarea A.
wealth: taonga N.
weapon: patu, raakau N.
weariness: ngenge, huuhi.
wearisome: hoohaa A.
weave: whatu-a, raranga.
web: tukutuku.
wed: maarena.
wedge: maakahi, matakahi,
   ora, weeti.
Wednesday: Wenerei N.
weed v.: ngaki-a.
weed n.: otaota, tarutaru.
week: wiki.
weep: tangi-hia.
weigh: paauna-tia.
weight: taimaha, toimaha,
   taumaha.
weir: paa.
welcome: poowhiri.
welcome!: haere mai!
   nau mai!
well: ora, pai A.
well (water): poka wai, puna.
Wellington: Pooneke L.
wen: ngene.
were: See under be.
west: uru, hauaauru, tai
   hauaauru.
wet: maakuu, haumaakuu.

whale: tohoraa, pakakee, paraaoa, weera *N*.
wharf: waapu *N*.
what?: aha-tia?
wheat: wiiti *N*.
wheedle: whakapati.
wheel: wiira *N*.
wheelbarrow: huripara *N*.
when: ina *verbal particle*.
when?: aa hea?, no naahea?
where?: hea? *L*.
whetstone: hoanga.
which?: tee(w)hea? *definitive*.
whip: whiu-a, wepu-a.
whirl: taawhiri-tia, koowhiri-a.
whirlpool: riporipo, aawhiowhio.
whirlwind: aawhiowhio.
whistle: whio, korowhiti, wiihara.
white: maa *A*, tea *A*.
White Island: Whakaari *L*.
whitebait: iinanga *N*.
whitish: koomaa.
whizz: mapu, huhuu.
who?: wai? *Pnl*.
whole: katoa *N*.
whose?: na/no wai?
why?: na te aha?, he aha . . . ai?
wicked: kino *A*.
wide: whaanui.
widow: pouaru *N*.
wife: wahine.
wild: maaka, koowao.
wilderness: kooraha.
will *n*.: wira *N*, oohaakii.
wind *v*.: pookai.
wind: hau.

winding: koopikopiko, aawhiowhio.
window: matapihi, mataaho *N*, wini *N*.
wine: waaina *N*.
wing: parirau *N*, paakau *N*, paihau.
wink: kamo, kimo, keko.
winnow: koowhiuwhiu.
winter: hootoke, takurua, makariri.
wipe: muru-a, (muku)muku-a, uku-ia.
wire: waea *N*.
wisdom: maatauranga, whakaaro-nui.
wise: maatau-ria, moohio-tia.
wish: hiahia-tia (ki), minamina, piirangi-tia.
witch: wahine maakutu.
witchcraft: maakutu-ria.
wither, withered: memenge *A*, pohe *A*.
withhold: kaiponu-hia, haakere-a.
witness: kaiwhakaatu.
witticism: pepeha.
wizard: tohunga maakutu.
wolf: wuruhi *N*.
woman: wahine (*pl.* waahine).
womb: koopuu *N*, takotoranga tamariki.
wonder: miiharo.
wonderful: whakamiiharo.
woo: aruaru.
wood: raakau *N*.
wood-hen: weka *N*.
woof (weft): aho.
wool: wuuru *N*.
woolly (of hair): kapu piripiri.

woolshed: wuuruheti *N*.
word: kupu *N*.
work: mahi-a.
world: ao.
worm: toke.
worn-out: ngawhewhe.
worry: maaharahara-tia.
worship: karakia-tia.
worthy: pai.
wounded: tuu *P*, kai-aa-kiko, whara *A*.
wrangle: rure-a, whakawaawaa-tia.
wrap up: takai-a.
wrath: riri-a, pukuriri *N*.

wreath: pare, koopare.
wrecked: pae-a, pakaru *P*.
wrench (tool): waawahi.
wrestle: mamau.
wriggle: korikori, okeoke.
wring: whakawiri-a, taatari-tia.
wrinkle: korukoru.
wrinkled: memenge, ngingio.
wrist: kawititanga o te ringaringa.
write: (tuhi)tuhi-a.
writhe: kowheta, okeoke, takawhetawheta.
wrong: hee *A*.

Y

yam: uwhi.
yard: marae.
yard (measure): iaari *N*.
yawn: kohera.
year: tau.
yearning: koonohi aroha, koingo.
yellow: koowhai, pungapunga.
yes: aae.

yesterday: i nanahi, no nanahi, i taainahi.
yield: tuku-a.
yoke: ioka.
young (animal): kuuao, punua.
young (bird): pii.
young (man): taitama.
young (woman): taitamaahine.
youth (time): taitamarikitanga.
youth (young person): taitama.

MAORI-ENGLISH

A

aa: and (after a time). **Aa hea? when?** (future) (LLM, 26.2).

a: of (LLM, 13.1–4, 17).

aa-ia: compel, drive.

aae: yes, say yes.

aha-tia: what?, do what?, be treated in what fashion?. **Aha ai?:** why?

ahakoa: although, nevertheless, notwithstanding.

ahau: I, me.

aahei: be able, have ability to.

ahi: fire.

Aahia: Asia.

ahiahi: afternoon, evening.

Ahitereiria: Australia.

aho: cord, fishing-line, line, woof.

ahu: move in some direction, face towards.

ahu-a, -ria: tend, foster. **Ahu-whenua:** cultivate, farm, work land.

ahu(ahu)-ngia: earth up, heap up.

aahua: appearance, character, form, likeness, shape, sort.

aahuareka: agreeable, pleasant; be delighted, interested.

aahuatanga: circumstance.

ahu-whenua: cultivate, farm, work land.

ai: a particle that follows the verb and indicates (a) that what has happened is a result of what has happened previously or (b) that the noun relativised by a relative clause is a non-subject. Not usually translated.

ai-tia: beget, cohabit, copulate, procreate.

aaianei: now, soon, at present.

aihi-kiriimi: ice cream.

aikiha: handkerchief.

aaio: calm, peace; be calm (of the sea), be at peace.

Airihi: Irish.

aitanga: descendant, progeny.

aituaa: accident, calamity, disaster, fate, misfortune, trouble; unfortunate, unlucky.

aakau: coast, sea-coast.

ake: upwards, henceforth. **Mo ake tonu atu:** for ever.

akiaki: red-billed gull (*Larus novaehollandiae scopulinus*).

akiaki-na: encourage, incite, urge.

aki-na: dash against, pound, beat on.

akiri-tia, aakirikiri-tia: reject, throw away.

ako-na: learn, instruct, teach (someone).

aakonga: scholar, pupil, learner.

akoranga: doctrine, teaching.

aaku: my (active, *pl.* possession) (LLM, 14.1–3).

aku: my (neutral, *pl.* possession) (LLM, 14.1–3, 15.4).

aakuanei: now, presently, soon, today.

Akuhata: August.

aamara: amble (of a horse).

amarara: umbrella.

Amerika: America, United States.

amo-hia: bear, carry on a litter, carry on the shoulder; bier, carrier, litter, stretcher.

amokura: red-tailed tropic-bird (*Phaethon rubricauda roseotincta*).

amuamu-tia: complain, grumble.

aana: third person singular (dominant) possessive adjective denoting *pl.* possession, his, her, of him, of her (LLM, 14.1–2).

anaa!: behold!, lo!; there (near you) is.

ana: cave, cavern; postposed verbal particle (LLM, 36); third person singular (neutral) possessive adjective denoting *pl.* possession, his, her (LLM, 14.1–2, 15.4); denoting a specific point in time, when (LLM, 8.1, 53.3).

anahera: angel.

anake: alone, only.

aniana: onion.

aanini: ache (of head), dizzy, giddy; dizziness, giddiness, headache.

aaniwaniwa: rainbow.

aanoo: as if, like (LLM, 37.14, 41.2).

anoo: again, still, too (LLM, 41.1, 51).

anuhe: caterpillar.

anga: face towards; husk, outer covering, shell.

anga-nui: opposite, square on to.

angaanga: head, skull.

anganga: aspect.

angiangi: thin.

ao-hia: gather up, scoop up.

ao: day (not night) light; cloud; earth, world. **Te Ao Maarama:** physical or mortal world as opposed to the spirit world.

apa: band of people (usually serving others).

apakura: dirge.

aperikota: apricot.

Aaperira: April.

apiapi: crowded.

aapiha: officer.

aapiti-ria: add to, supplement, add, join; fight at close quarters; gorge, pass.

aapitireihana: arbitration.

apo-hia: gather together, grasp, take, heap up; avaricious.

apoapo-hia: collect.

aapoopoo: tomorrow.

aaporo: apple.

aapotoro: apostle.

apu-a, -ria: cram food into mouth, gorge; heap up, heap upon, cover over; force one's way into the ground.

aapuru-a: crowd one upon another, suppress thoughts; be covered with (e.g., blood).

araa: namely, that is to say.

ara: arise, wake, rise up; path, road, track, way; amniotic water.

arahi-na: conduct, lead, guide, lead.

aarai-a, -tia: block, hinder, obstruct, ward off, prevent; barricade, curtain, hindrance, obstacle, screen, veil, wind-break.

aarai ahi: fire-screen, fender.

aarani: orange.

aranga: become famous, be celebrated, become known.

araara: trevally (*Usacaranx lutescens*).

arataki-na: conduct, lead.

aarau: entangle, entangled.

arawhata: bridge, ladder, stairs.

areare: overhanging, arched, clear of obstruction, open.

arero: tongue.

arewhana: elephant.

ariki: chief, lord. **Te Ariki**, the Lord.

aro-ngia: front (of a person), bowels, kidney fat; be inclined towards, face, turn towards; inclination, desire.

aroaro: front of a person, polite term for genital area. **I te aroaro o:** in the presence of.

aroha-ina, -tia: affection, compassion, pity, sympathy, love, like, grace, regret, regretful, yearning; to love, feel compassion, sympathy, or love for.

aronui: desire, inclination; right opposite, directly forward, straight.

aropereina: aeroplane, aircraft, plane.

aru(aru)-mia: chase, follow, pursue; woo, court; interrupt.

aruhe: edible rhizome of bracken, fernroot.

aata: altar; quite, carefully, thoroughly.

ata: dawn, morning, reflected image, shadow.

aataahua: beautiful, handsome, pretty.

aatamira: admiral.

atamira: bier, platform, stage.

ata-poo: dawn.

atarau: moonlight.

atatuu: dawn.

atawhai-tia: kind, generous, liberal; show kindness, be liberal, foster, take care of; generosity, kindness. **Tamaiti atawhai:** foster child.

ate: liver.

atea: clear, free from obstruction.

ateha: assessor (legal).

aatete-tia: oppose, resist.

ato-hia: thatch, to thatch.

atu: direction away from speaker (LLM, 21.2); marker of comparative degree.

atua: god, superhuman; unnatural, supernatural.

au: I, me; bark (of dog); current, rapid; sound (of sleep).

aua! I don't know!

aua: herring, sprat.

auahi: smoke; to spread (as smoke does).

auee!: alas!, ah me!, oh dear!, woe is me!

auee-tia: groan, howl, lament, mourn, scream, squeal, wail.

aukaha: lashing, binding.

aurara: clutch.

aurere: groan, moan.

autaaia: fellow.

auwahine: sister-in-law.

awa: channel, creek, river.

awa-kari: moat, ditch, drain.

awa-keri: moat, ditch, drain.

awa-mate: moat, back-water.

aawangawanga: anxious, disquieted, distressed, undecided; anxiety, distress.

awatea: day, daylight.

awau: I, me.

awaawa: groove, valley.

awe kootuku: white-heron plume.

awe: soot.

aweke-tia: dawdle; falsify, prevaricate.

aawhaa: gale, storm.

awheo: halo.

Aawherika: Africa.

awhi-tia: beset, besiege; embrace.

aawhina-tia: assist, help, succour; assistance, help.

aawhio: go by a roundabout way, wander; roundabout, winding, circuitous.

aawhiowhio: whirlpool, whirlwind, winding.

E

e: non-past tense-marker (LLM, 8.1, 30.1); if, when (LLM, 48.2); by (agent) (LLM, 7.1); indefinite article (Northern dialect).

ea: avenged, paid, requited; emerge (after immersion).

ehu-a: bail out liquids, dash out water; turbid.

eka: acre.

eekara: eagle.

eke-a, -ngia: board a vessel, go on to a marae, mount (horse, vehicle).

emi(emi): assembled, gathered together.

eenei: these (LLM, 3).

engari: but, but rather, rather.

epa-ina: pelt, throw; objection.

eetahi: certain, particular, more, other, some (LLM, 15.2).

ewe: afterbirth.

H

haa: breath, flavour, taste.
haa-kore: insipid, tasteless.
hae: (*See* hahae).
haaea: (*See* hahae).
haeana: harpoon, iron.
hae(hae)-a: cut, slash, slice; groove.
haere-a: go, proceed, travel; journey.
haere atu: go away. Haere mai: come, welcome.
haere-a-waewae: go on foot, walk. Haaereere: roam, stroll, wander.
haahaa: search, seek.
hahae, haaea: jealous; jealousy, envy; slit, slash.
hahani: (*See* hanihani).
hahau-tia, (haaua): hew.
haahi: church (sect), religion.
hahu-a: disinter, exhume.
hai: ace (in cards); scythe.
haihana: sergeant.
haika: anchor.
haina-tia: sign, affix signature.
Haina: China.
Hainamana: Chinese.
haira: scythe.
haaka: jug.
haka-a: dance, particularly the war-dance.
hakahaka: low, short.
haakarameta: sacrament.
hake: crooked; hunchback.
hakeke: fungus.

haakere-a: stingy; withhold, stint, begrudge, keep for oneself.
haki: flag; cheque.
haakiki: overbearing.
haku: kingfish (*Seriola grandis*).
haku(haku)-a: complain of, find fault with, grumble at.
hama: hammer.
haamama: bawl, shout; gaping, open, empty.
haamanu: ammunition; cartridge-belt, bandolier.
haamarara: umbrella.
haamene-tia: summon (legal); summons (legal).
haami: jam.
Haamoa: Samoa.
haamu: jam.
hamu: gather things that are thinly scattered, glean.
hamuhamu: eat scraps.
hamumu: mutter.
hamupaka: humbug, sham.
Haamutana: Hamilton.
haanarete: hundredweight.
hanawiti: sandwich.
hane-a: confounded, shamed, silenced.
hanihani: disparage, speak ill of; disparagement.
haanihi: harness.
Haanuere: January.
hanumi: merged, mixed with.
hanga-a: build, create, fashion, make.

hangahanga: frivolous, of no account.

haangai: across, confronting, opposite. **Toki haangai:** adze (as opposed to axe).

hangarau: deceive, fool.

haangii: earth-oven.

hangoro: slack, loose; slip (of a knot).

haangorongoro: slack, loose.

haangorungoru: hanging in folds, wrinkled.

haanguu: dumb, quiet, silent, not talkative.

haangurunguru: grumbling.

hao-a: catch in a net, encircle, enclose, net.

haaona: horn.

haora: hour.

haapa: harp.

hapa: supper; be passed over in the apportionment of anything, be in need, be omitted; gone by.

haapai-nga, -ngia: elevate, raise, lift up.

haapara: shovel.

hapareta: separator (used to separate milk from cream).

haapati: sabbath.

hape: club-footed, crooked, lame.

haapu: shop (Taranaki dialect).

hapuu: conceive, become pregnant, pregnant; subtribe.

haapuku: groper (*Polyprion oxygeneios*).

hara: crime, offence, sin, wrong; commit a crime, to sin, make a mistake, miss.

Hara mai: come; welcome! = **haere mai** .

harakeke: New Zealand flax (*Phormium tenax*).

hararei: holiday.

harawene: envious, jealous; envy, jealousy.

hari: delighted, elated, glad, happy, merry; joy, happiness; rejoice.

hari-a: bear, carry.

hariata: chariot.

haarikeehi: hard case, rascal.

haaroo: scrape, scutch (as flax).

haro: harrow.

harore: fungus of various kinds including mushroom.

haruru: resound, reverberate, rumble.

haatakeehi: hard case, rascal.

Haatarei: Saturday.

haate: heart card; shirt.

haatea: faded.

hau: air, breeze, wind; dew; spread (as news).

haaua: (*See* **hahau**).

hauaa: crippled, lame; cripple, disabled person.

hauangi: cool.

hauaauru: west, west wind. **Tai hauaauru:** western area of the North Island.

hauhake-tia: dig up a root crop.

hauhakenga: harvest.

hauhau: cool; cool air, fresh air, draught; beat, smite, strike; chop, hew.

hauhunga: frost.

haukuu: dew.

haumaakuu: be-dewed, damp, wet.

haaunga: besides, not counting, excepting.

haunga: odour, unpleasant smell, stench, stink.

hauora: breeze; health.

haupapa-tia: ambush, lie in wait for; frost, ice.

haurangi: drunk, intoxicated.

hauraro: low.

haurokuroku: uncertain, unsettled, variable.

haututuu: troublesome.

hau(w)area: weak of will, ineffective, listless, lethargic.

hawa: chipped.

hawai: an edible fungus that grows on trees.

haaware: saliva, spittle.

haawareware: dribbling; slimy.

haawata: delirious; mutter.

haawera: shovel.

haawini: servant.

haawhe-tia: half; halve.

haawhe-kaaihe, half-caste.

hee: in error, mistaken, wrong; error, fault, offence; do wrong, fail.

he: a, an, some (LLM, 2.1); nominal predicate marker (LLM, 4).

hea?: where?; hare; ploughshare; portion, share. **Aa hea?:** when? (in the future).

heahea: foolish, idiotic, silly.

heamana: chairperson.

heheu, heu-a: clear away (as scrub), shave (as beard); razor.

hei: at, in, on (future) (LLM, 11.4, 12.1, 17); hay; a neck pendant. **ka hei koe!:** you will get what you deserve!

heihei: chook, fowl, hen.

heka: mouldy.

hekaheka: mildew.

heke-a: descend, dismount, disembark, go down, subside; migrate; migration; rafter.

heekena, heekene: second.

hekeretari: secretary.

heketanga: descent, downward slope.

heketea: hectare.

heeki: egg.

hema: bevel, chamfer; left hand.

hee-manawa: impatience, exhaustion, lack of breath.

hemo: dead, die; miss a mark; be all done, all used up; break wind, fart. **Hemo i te kai:** hungry.

heneti: cent. **Pai heneti:** per cent.

heoi: accordingly. **Heoi anoo:** enough, enough said, so much for that.

heepara: shepherd.

Hepetema: September.

heera: sail *n.*

heeramana: sailor.

here-a: long lance or spear used formerly to spear pigeons; to spear with such.

here(here)-a, -ngia: bind, tie, tie up; oblige, put under an obligation; string, cord, binding; bunch; captive, prisoner, slave. **Mau herehere:** taken prisoner. **Whare herehere:** jail.

here-taniwha: clove-hitch.

hereni, herengi: shilling.

heri: carry. = **hari.**

heru-a: comb, to comb.

heeteri: sentry.

heeti: shed.

heu: (*See* **heheu**).

heuheu-tia: brushwood; clear away (as weeds, scrub), scatter (as people).

hewa: deluded, under a false impression.

hia-: prefix indicating desire, inclination, wish.

hii-a: fish with a line; draw up, raise, lift on a line. **Hii te ata:** break day.

hiia: (*See* **hihii** and **hii-a**).

hiahia-tia: crave, desire, inclination, want, wish for.

hiainu: thirst; thirsty.

hiakai: hunger, hungry, appetite.

hiako: bark, hide, peel, rind, skin.

hiamoe: drowsy, sleepy, sleepiness.

hiianga-tia: deceiving, dishonest, mischievous; deceit, deception; deceive.

hiato: compact, gathered together in small compass.

hihii, hiia: draw up, pull up (as a fish on a line, one's clothes).

hii(hii): hiss.

hihi: ray, sunbeam; antennae, feelers, tentacle.

hihira-tia: shy, wary of.

hihiri: energetic.

hika-ia: female genitals; copulate; generate fire by fire-plough method. **E hika!:** familiar term of address (East Coast dialects).

hiikaka: impetuous, over-eager, rash.

hikareti: cigarette. **Kai hikareti:** smoke tobacco.

hiki-tia: adjourn a meeting; carry in the arms, lift, nurse a baby.

hikipene: sixpence.

hiko: flash; electricity, lightning; move randomly.

hikohiko: flash repeatedly, twinkle; disjointed, incomplete (of genealogy).

hiikoi: step, stride.

hiku: tail of fish.

hiku-awa: head of a river.

hiimene: hymn.

himu: hip.

hina: grey hair; shine with a pale light.

hinahina: grey haired, pale; a tree (*Melicytus ramiflorus*) (Eastern dialects) = **maahoe.**

hiinaki: eel-pot.

hinapoouri: dark(ness); sad(ness).

hinengaro: mind (as opposed to body).

hiinota: synod.

hinu: fat, grease, oil.

hinga: beaten, defeated; fall from an upright position (as a felled tree).

hinganga: defeat, falling, overthrow.

hingareti: singlet.

hipa: go by, pass, turn aside; exceed in length.

hipi: sheep. **Miiti hipi:** mutton.

hiipoki-na: cover, covered.

hipora: roughly made flax mats or baskets.

hiira: shield.

hira: seed (Ngaati Porou).

hiraka: silk.

hiirau-tia: entangled; entangle, trip up.

hiirawerawe: irksome, painful. **Hiirawerawe i te kata:** laugh till it hurts.

hiirearea: indistinct (of sound).

hiirere: gush, spurt.

hiiri-tia: seal, stamp.

hiriwa: silver.

hiirori: stagger, unsteady.

hiita: cedar; heater.

hiiteki: hop.

hiiti: sheet.

hiitimi: marbles (game).

hiitoko: hop.

hiitori: history, tradition.

hiwa: watchful, alert.

hiwi: ridge; jerk a line.

ho(o)-: a root that occurs only prefixed to the particles atu, mai, ake. (*See* **hoake, hoatu, hoomai**).

hoo: spade.

hoa: accomplice, companion, friend, mate, partner, spouse.

hoariri: enemy. **Hoa-whawhai:** antagonist, opponent.

hoake: go on, move on.

hoanga: grindstone, whetstone.

hoari: sword.

hoariri: antagonist, enemy.

hoatu: contribute, give (away); set out, move off.

hoe-a: oar, paddle.

hoeha: saucer.

hoohaa: bored, tired, impatient with; wearisome. **Hoohaa!:** exclamation of anger at someone's annoying behaviour.

hooha: saucer.

hoohi: saucer.

hohipera: hospital.

hohipere: hospital.

hoohonu: deep; esoteric.

hohoro: fast, quick, hasty, nimble, swift; speed, swiftness.

hohou-tia: (houhia): bind. **Hohou rongo:** peace-making.

hooia: soldier.

hoihere: lacebark (*Hoheria populnea*) (Northern dialect).

hooiho: horse.

hoihoi: noisy; contradict. **Hoihoi!:** shut up (that noise)!

hookai: brace, stay; go briskly, proceed smartly, dash.

hookeke: a fungus (*Auricularia auricula-judaea*).

hoki: also, too (LLM, 47).

hoki-a: return, go back, turn back.

hoko(hoko)-na: barter, buy, exchange, purchase, redeem, sell; sale, trade. **Kai-hoko:** buyer, seller, trader.

hokomirimiri: stroke.

hokorete: chocolate.

hoomai: contribute, give.

honi: honey.

hono-a: add, connect, graft, join, splice.

hoonore: honour.

hongi(hongi)-a: smell, sniff; press noses as a form of greeting.

hoopa: sofa.

hoopane: saucepan.

hope: hips, waist. **Ringa hope:** hands on hips.

hopi: soap.

hopohopo: apprehensive, fearful, overawed.

hopu-kia, -kina: catch, seize, snatch; surprise.

hoopua: deep pool.

horera: sorrel.

hori: false.

horihori: falsehood, lie; gone by.

hori-a: cut, slit; brand a beast by ear-marking.

hooro: hall.

horo-a: break (of a wave), crumble (of a bank), fall (of a fortress); escape, flee, run away; landslip.

horoi-a: cleanse, scour, scrub, wash.

horomi-a: devour, gulp, swallow.

hooruu: red ochre.

horu: grunt, snort, sob.

hoota: shot.

hooteera: hotel, public-house, tavern.

hootoke: winter.

hotu(hotu): pant, sob.

hoou: fresh, new, recent.

hou-a: force downwards or under; enter.

houhere: lacebark (*Hoheria* spp.).

houhi: lacebark (*Hoheria* spp.).

houhia: (*See* **hohou-tia**).

houhou-a: chop in pieces; peck holes in.

houi: lacebark (*Hoheria* spp.) (Eastern dialects).

houkeke: churlish.

hooura: soda.

huu: boil, bubble, hiss; eruption (volcanic); shoe; cry of bittern, rail, etc.

hua: abound, bear fruit, wax (of moon); egg, fruit, roe.

hua-ia: lever up, steer.

hua-ina: to name.

huahua: pimple.

huaki-na: attack, charge, rush at; open, uncover. **Huaki te ata:** day breaks.

hua-kore: unfruitful.

huanui: road, street.

huaanga: kin, relative, relation (not close).

huango: asthma.

huarahi: road, street, track.

huare: spittle.

hue: gourd plant (*Lagenaria* sp.).

huuhaa: (*See* **huuwhaa**).

huuhi: discomfort, weariness.

huhuu: hiss, whizz.

huhu-a: strip off an outer covering, make bare; an edible grub (*Prionoplus reticularis*).

huhua-kore: causeless.

huhuatange: advantage.

huhuka: foaming.

huhuti, (huti-a): pluck a bird; hoist, pull up (e.g., a line).

hui(hui)-a: assemble, congregate, add, collect, gather, put together, throng; assembly, gathering, meeting.

huihuinga: assemblage, crowd, meeting.

huuiki: exhausted (of land).

huiti: suit of clothes.

huuka: slasher.

huka: foam, frost, froth, snow, sugar.

hukahuka: thrum, tassel; foam, froth.

hukapapa: frost.

hukarere: snow.

huke-a: excavate, open (an earth-oven), uncover.

huukeke: convulsion; stagger.

hukehuke: rootings (as by a pig).

huki(huki): avenge (a death); roast on a spit; stick in, transfix; contract, convulse, twitch; convulsion.

huukiki: shiver.

huumarie, huumaarire: beautiful, comely, handsome.

huna-a, -ia: conceal, hide; destroy, destroyed.

hunaonga: daughter-in-law, son-in-law.

Hune: June.

hunu(hunu)-a: char, grill, scorch, singe.

hungarei: father-in-law, mother-in-law.

hungawai: father-in-law, mother-in-law.

hupa: soup.

huupeke-tia: contract, bend of arm or leg.

huupirimi kooti: supreme court.

hura-hia: discover, uncover, expose.

Huurae: July.

Huurai: Jew.

huu-repo: bittern (*Botaurus poiciloptilus*).

huuri: jury.

huri-hia: convert, discuss, invert, overthrow, overturn, turn inside out, turn the back, turn upside down; grind (flour), turn; trump (in playing cards).

hurihuri: roll, turn over and over. **Puu hurihuri:** revolver.

huripara: wheelbarrow.

huripoki: cover over; turn (something) upside down or over.

huru-a: contract, draw in, gird on (e.g., a belt).

hurupoki: cover over.

huutia: (*See* **huhuti**).

huutoitoi: dishevelled.

huutu: suit of clothes.
hutu: a shrub (*Ascarina lucida*).
hutupaoro, hutupooro: football.

huu(w)ai: cockle (*Chione stutchburyi*).
huuware: saliva.
huuwhaa: thigh.

I

i(i): past tense marker (LLM, 8); at, from, in, on, position marker (LLM, 6, 6.2, 10.21, 11.3, 17.231, 38.4); object marker (LLM, 32.21); cause marker (LLM, 32.23).
ii: ferment, go sour; stirred (of emotions).
ia: he, she, it; each; current.
Ia....ia: every.
iaari: yard measure.
ihi(ihi)-a: shudder, thrill (especially at a moving performance of some Maori song or dance); spiritual power derived from one's Maori heritage; ray of sunlight.
Iihipa: Egypt.
iho: kernel, pith; umbilical cord; downwards (LLM, 21.41).
ihu: nose, snout; bow (of a canoe), prow.
Ihu: Jesus.
ika: fish; victim of war.
ikeike: lofty.
inaa: if and when, inasmuch as, since, because, when.

inaaianei: now, at present.
inahea: (*See* **ina(w)hea**).
inaina: bask in sun.
inaki-tia: crowd one upon another, overlap.
inakuanei: just now, recently.
inakuara: a little while ago.
iinanga: whitebait.
inaapoo: last night.
inarapa: rubber.
Iinia: India.
inihi: inch.
inoi-a: appeal, entreaty, favour, prayer; ask for, beg for, beseech, pray, request.
inu-mia: drink.
Ingarangi: England.
Ingarihi: English; Englishman.
ingiki: ink.
ingoa: name, namesake, title.
io(io): muscle, nerve, sinew; strand (of hair, fibre), warp (vertical thread in weaving).
ioka: yoke.
ipo: lover, paramour, sweetheart.
ipu: bottle, calabash, gourd.
ira(ira): freckle, mole or other natural mark on skin.
iraamutu: nephew, niece.

irawaru: incest.
iri-a: hang, suspend.
iroiro: maggot, thread-worm.
itarete: interest, usury.
Iitari: Italy.
Iitariana: Italian.
iti: little, small.

Iti haere: diminish, dwindle.
Iti iho: less.
iwa: nine.
iwi: bone; nation, people, race of people, tribe.
iwi-kore: feeble, languid, listless.

K

kaa: burn (of fire).
ka(a): verbal particle marking beginning of a new action (LLM, 8).
kaha: ability, effort, energy, power, strength, force; able, strong enough; binding, lashing rope.
kahaki-na: bolt (of a horse).
kaaheru: spade.
kahika(tea): white pine (*Podocarpus excelsum*).
kahikaatoa: tea-tree (*Leptospermum scoparium*) (Northern dialect).
kaahiti: gazette.
kahitua: bivalve mollusc (*Amphidesma subtriangulatum*) (Eastern dialects) = **tuatua**.
kaahiwahiwa: dark.
kaaho: cask, barrel.
kaho: roof-batten or purlin.
kaahore: no; negative marker (LLM, 20.1, 20.3) (Northern dialects).
kaahu: harrier hawk (*Circus gouldi*).

kaahui: flock (e.g., sheep), herd. **Kaahui ariki:** collective term for the descendants of the Maori kings.
kahukahu: caul.
Kahukura: rainbow.
kahurangi: jewel, precious possession.
kai: food, eat.
kai-: prefix indicating human agency.
kai: at, present position (Eastern dialects); lest.
kaiaa: thief.
kai-aa-kiko: wounded.
kai-amo: bearer, carrier, porter.
kaiapo: greedy, covetous.
kai-arahi: guide, leader.
kai-aawhina: assistant.
kaihana: cousin.
kaaihe: ass, donkey.
kaihoro: glutton, gluttony, greedy, greed; eat ravenously.
kaikaa: eager, impatient; hurry, rush.
kaikai-wai-uu: betray.
kai-koorero: speaker.
kaimahi: servant, worker.

kaimahi-paamu: farmer.

kai-maakete: auctioneer.

kaimata: fresh (of vegetables), green (of fruit), uncooked, unripe, unseasoned (of timber).

kai-mau: bearer.

kaainga: abode, address, dwelling-place, home, residence, village.

kai-nga: eat; food.

kai-ngaakau-tia: prize, treasure, place great value on.

kaiponu-hia: avaricious, stingy, withhold.

kaipuke: ship.

kai-pupiri: holder.

kai-riiwhi: reliever, successor.

kai-ruuri: surveyor.

kai-taa: printer.

kai-tirotiro: inspector.

kai-tono: sender.

kai-tuhituhi: scribe, writer.

kai-urungi: pilot.

kai-waiata: singer, vocalist.

kai-whakaako: teacher.

kai-whakamaaori: interpreter.

kai-whakaora: saviour.

kai-whakaatu: witness.

kai-whakawaa: adjudicator, judge.

kai-whiriwhiri: selector.

kaakaa: parrot.

kakaa: hot, red hot.

kaka: fibre; clothing, garment.

kaakahi: freshwater mussel (*Diplodon lutulentus*).

kaakaho: culm of toetoe or pampas grass, reed.

kaakahu-ria: cloak, garment; clothe, dress.

kakai: nibble, bite frequently (as fish).

kakama: capable, fast, nimble, quick, swift.

kaakano: berry, grain, seed.

kakano: grain in timber.

ka(ka)pi, kapia: cover completely, occupy fully, close (as a door, gate, eyes).

kakara: aromatic, fragrant; fragrance, odour, savour, scent.

ka(ka)ramuu: shrubs or small trees (*Coprosma* spp.).

kaakaariki: green colour; melon; parakeet; small green lizard (*Nautilus elegans*).

ka(ka)ro-hia: parry, ward off.

kakati, (katia): bite, sting; acrid, sour, bitter.

kakau: handle, stalk.

kakawa: perspiration, sweat.

kake-a: ascend, climb.

kakii: neck.

kaamaka: rock.

kaamera: camel; camera.

kamikami: (*See* **kamokamo**).

kamo: eyelash; wink.

kamokamo: a kind of marrow whose immature fruit are a much-favoured vegetable. **Kamikami:** is a corruption often heard.

kamupene: company (commercial).

kamupeniheihana: compensation.

kamupuutu: gumboot.

kaamura: carpenter.

kanae: mullet (*Mugil cephalus*).

kana(kana): stare wildly.

kanapa: bright, glare, glisten.

kanapihi: cannabis.

kanapu: lightning.

kaanara: candle; colonel.

Kaanata: Canada.

kaaneihana: carnation.

kani: saw.

kanikani: dance.

kaaniwha: barb.

kanohi: countenance, eye, face. **Kanohi wera:** those who work in the kitchen at tribal gatherings.

kanoi: strand of rope.

kaanuka: a tree, teatree. (Usually said to be restricted to *Leptospermum ericoides*, but probably an eastern dialect form of maanuka and hence referring to both *Leptospermum* spp.).

kaanga: corn, maize. **Kaanga koopiro, kaanga wai:** corn that has been steeped in running water for several weeks before being cooked as a porridge.

kanga-a: abuse, curse, insult.

kaao: no.

kaokao: rib, side.

kapa: line, rank, row; copper, penny.

kapakapa: beat (of heart), flap (of flag, wings), throb.

kaapata: cupboard.

kape-a: eyebrow; copy, replica; copy, duplicate, reproduce; leave out, omit, pass by;

push away, reject.

kaapehu: compass.

kaapene: captain.

kaapeta: carpet.

kaapeti: cabbage; carpet.

kaapia: gum, resin.

kapi: fully occupied, covered.

kapiti: crevice, gorge; clenched, joined together, obstructed.

kaapoo: blind, without sight.

kapo-hia: seize, snatch.

kaponga: a tree fern (*Cyathea dealbata*) = **ponga**.

kaporeihana: incorporation.

kapo-wai: dragonfly.

kapua: cloud.

kapu(kapu): adze; hollow of the hand, sole of the foot; curly. **Kapu mahora:** wavy. **Kapu maawhatu:** in distinct curls. **Kapu piripiri:** woolly.

kapunga: handful, palm of the hand; scoop up with both hands.

kaapura: fire (Northern dialects).

karaa: basalt.

kara: colour; flag.

karaahe: glass.

karaehe: glass.

karaahi: class (school); glass.

karahiini: kerosene.

karahipi: scholarship.

karaaihe: grass.

Karaiti, (Te): Christ.

karaka: clock; clerk; a tree (*Corynocarpus laevigatus*).

karakata: pheasant.

karakia-tia: chant, charm, incantation, prayer, spell;

pray, recite a spell. **Whare karakia:** church (building).

kaaramuramu: shrubs or small trees (*Coprosma* spp.) (Tuuhoe dialect).

karanga-hia, -tia: call out, hail, shout, summon; ceremonial call of welcome onto a marae. **Pari kaarangaranga:** echo, place that echoes.

kaarangi(rangi): doubtful, restless, unsettled; irritating, provoking.

karanguu: shrubs or small trees (*Coprosma* spp.).

karaaone: crown.

kara-one: draw hoe.

kaarapa: glance, look askance; squinting.

karapa: crupper (harness); squinting, blind.

karapoti-a: encircle, hedge in, surround.

karapu: club (association); glove.

kararehe: animal, beast, quadruped.

karaati: garage; grant.

kaarau: dredge.

karauna: crown (government).

karawhaea: harrow, scarifier.

karawhiu-a: flail, whip.

kare-a: lash (of a whip), whip a top; ripple; darling; to desire, long for.

kaarearea: sparrowhawk (*Falco novaeseelandiae*).

karekare: surf, breaking waves.

kareko: calico.

kaaremu: plug.

karengo: an edible seaweed

(*Porphyria columbina*).

kareparaoa: cauliflower.

karepe: grape.

karere: messenger.

kaareti: carrot; college; carriage (of train).

kaarewa: buoy, float.

kaari: card; garden.

Kariki: Greek.

kariri: cartridge.

karoro: gull (*Larus dominicanus*).

karu: eye.

kaarua: grapnel.

karukaru: rag, tattered garment.

karu-paatene: wax-eye (*Zosterops lateralis*).

kaata: cart.

kata-ina: laugh, laugh at.

kaatene: curtain.

kaati!: cease, hush!, enough!

kati-a: blocked up, obstructed; shut.

katikati: bite frequently, champ, nibble.

katikiihama: catechism.

Katimana: Scotsman.

kaatipa: constable.

kato-hia: pick flowers, pluck.

katoa: all, every, total, whole.

kaatoretore: glimmer.

(ka)kau, kauria: swim.

kau: cow; a particle indicating absence of other factors, only. **Tuu kau:** naked.

kau-amo: litter, stretcher.

kauanga: ford, river crossing.

kauhoa: bier, carry on a litter.

kauhoe-tia: swim.

kaukau: bathe, wash.

kaumaatua-tia: old (of people); elder (male); become adult or elderly.

kaunihera: council.

kaaunga: hermit crab.

kaupae: step of ladder.

kaupapa: level floor, platform, stage; matter for discussion, topic, policy.

kaupare-a: avert.

kaupoai: cowboy.

kaauru: head of a tree.

kaauta: cookhouse.

kau-taahoe: swim.

kaute: account, bill.

kau(w)ae: jaw, chin.

kauwhau-tia: preach, recite; sermon.

kawa: acid, bitter, distasteful, sour, unpalatable.

kaawai: ancestry, genealogy, lineage, pedigree.

kaawana: governor; swan.

kaawanatanga: government.

kawau: shag (*Phalocrocorax* spp.).

kawe-a: bear, carry, fetch; handle (of a basket or kit), strap.

kawe kee: change, convert, distort, pervert.

kawenata: covenant, testament.

kawenga: load, pack, burden.

kaawiri-tia: twist.

kawiti(witi): dwindle, narrow, taper. **Kawititanga o te ringaringa:** wrist.

ka(w)haki-na: abduct, carry off by force; bolt (of a horse).

kaawhe: calf.

kawhe: coffee.

kaawhena: coffin.

kee: particle marking a change of state or an unexpected outcome (LLM, 22.3). **Kawe kee:** change, pervert.

kea: phlegm, semen, snot; mountain parrot (*Nestor notabilis*).

keha: flea; turnip.

keehi: case (legal).

kehokeho: an intensive adverb. **Maarama kehokeho:** very clear, transparent.

keehua: ghost, goblin, strange, unexplained phenomenon; traffic cop.

kei te: if followed by a verb, marks a present continuous tense.

kei: particle indicating present position, at (LLM, 11.2, 12.1); stern (of a vessel); lest (LLM, 8.1, 29, 33.2).

keka: fungus.

keekee: armpit. **Matua keekee:** aunt, uncle, relative of first ascending generation.

kekee: creak.

keke: cake.

kekeno: seal (animal).

keko: squint, wink.

keemihi: chemist.

keena, keene: can, pannikin.

keenana: canon.

kenepuru: silt.

keo: peak.

kereeme: claim *n*.

kerepei: clod (of earth).

kerepi: grape.

kereruu: pigeon.
keri-a: dig.
kete: basket, especially a woven flax kit.
ketekete: express surprise by clicking tongue against the palate or teeth.
keeti: gate.
ketoketo: maggot.
ketu(ketu)-a: root (as a pig does), scratch up.
keu-a: pull trigger of a gun.
ki te: when followed by a verb **ki te** marks the infinitive (LLM, 32.14); when preceded by a passive verb **ki te** marks the instrument and will be translated 'with' or 'by' (LLM, 32.15).
kii: full.
ki: particle indicating movement towards, to (LLM, 6, 6.1, 11.1).
kii-a: say, speak, word.
kia: verbal particle marking desiderative aspect (LLM, 8.1–2), in order to, so that.
kiiaka: calabash, gourd.
kiaano: not yet.
kiha(kiha): gasp, pant.
kihi-a: kiss.
kihikihi: cicada.
kiihini: kitchen.
kikii: confined, crowded, full, tight.
kiki: spur (harness); gig (vehicle).
kiki-a: kick.
ki(ki)ni: nip, pinch.
kiko: flesh, female genitals, kernel (of a nut).

kikokiko: flesh.
kikowhiti: forearm.
kimi-hia: look for, search, seek.
kimo: blink, wink.
kina: sea-egg, sea-urchin, *Echinus*.
kini-tia: nip, pinch.
kino: bad, damaged, evil, ugly, wicked; dislike, harm, hate; evil, harm, problem.
kiingi: king.
kiingitanga: kingdom.
kiore: rat. **Kiore iti:** mouse.
kipa: spur (harness).
kiirehe: dog.
kiri: bark, skin. **Kiri kau:** naked.
Kirihimete: Christmas.
kirikiri: gravel.
kirikiti: cricket game.
kiriimi: cream.
kirimini: agreement (legal).
kiripaka: flint.
kiritea: fair, pale, white (of complexion).
kiritona: wart; stye.
kitaa: guitar.
kita: intensive adverb. **Mau kita:** firm, tight.
kite-a: discern, discover, find, know, perceive, see, understand.
kitenga: sight, vision.
kiwi: *Apteryx* spp.
kiiwha: discs (agricultural), disc harrow.
kiiwhi: disc harrow.
koo: beyond, farther, further; traditional digging-stick; term of address to young girls.

ko: grammatical particle marking nominal predicates (LLM, 4.3–4, 17.1–2) and subjects in focus (LLM, 38.2–3).

koa: elated, exultant, glad, happy; joy, delight; rejoice.

koaea: choir.

kooanga: spring (season).

koara-tia: crack, cracked, split open; force open.

kooaro: inverted, inside out, right round. **Huri kooaro:** turn inside out.

koata: quarter.

koati: goat.

kooauau: flute.

koe: thou, you (*sing.*).

koea: square (tool); square gin.

koeke: adult, old person.

kooemi: flinch.

koha: defect; donation, gift, offering, present; parting instruction, good advice.

koohamo: back of the head.

kohara: split open.

koohari-tia: crush, mash.

kooheru: herring scad, yellowtail (*Caranx koheru*).

kohi: consumption, tuberculosis.

kohi(kohi)-a: collect, gather, gather in (a rope), pick.

koohikohiko: do something irregularly (a bit here and there); quiver, shimmer (as hot air).

koohine: girl.

kohu: fog, haze, mist.

koohua-tia: pot; cook by boiling.

koohue-tia: pot; cook by boiling.

kohuki: transfix; spit.

kohukohu: chickweed, moss; curse.

koohumuhumu: murmur, whisper.

koohungahunga: crushed.

koohure-a: turn up (as earth, an eyelid); conspicuous, showing.

koohuri: sapling.

koohuru-tia: murder.

koi: sharp; spike, splinter; lest (*See* **kei**).

koia: therefore, so, hence.

koikoi: prickly, thorn.

koinaa: there (near you), there is.

koinei: here, here is.

koinga: edge of a cutting instrument, tip.

koingo: yearning.

koingo-tia: fret, grieve, yearn.

kooipuipu: blistered, overcast.

kooiwi: bone (human), skeleton.

kookaa: mother (biological).

kookako: New Zealand crow (*Callaeas cinerea*).

kooke: cork.

kookii: shark liver prepared for eating.

koki: angle, corner.

kookiri-tia: attack, charge, dart forward; launch, spear, thrust; set (a sail).

kokoo: gurgle.

koko: corner.

koko-a: scoop.

kokonga: corner.

kokopi, (kopia): doubled together, clamped on (as legs when riding a horse), closed (as hand).

kokoroihe: cockroach.

kokoru(tanga): bay, cove, bight.

kookota: edible bivalve mollusc (*Mesodesma australe*).

kokoti: cut, prune, reap.

kookoowai: ochre, red, red ochre.

koomaa: pale, whitish.

koomae: blighted.

koomaoa: ulcerated.

komata: nipple.

komihana: commission.

koomiri-a: pick, select.

komiti: committee. **Komiti whakahaere:** management committee.

komutu-a: surprise, ambush.

konaa: there (near you).

kona: abdomen, lower belly.

konana: slant.

koonata: cornet.

koonatu: crush, mash.

koonehunehu: drizzle.

konei: here, this place.

kooneke: sledge.

konihi: graze, pass near; stealthy; go stealthily.

koonini: fruit of kootukutuku (*Fuchsia excorticata*).

kono: a small basket for cooked food.

koonohete: concert.

koonohi: regret, regretful; yearning.

konotaraka: contract, contractor.

koo-nui: thumb, big toe.

kongakonga: crumb; crumbled.

koongangi: creak.

koonguu: cloudy, overcast.

kopa: crippled, lame; bent, folded.

koopae: broadside on.

koopaki-na: enfold, envelop, fold; envelope, husk.

koopako: head (back of).

kopakopa: creased, wrinkled.

koopani-a: enclose, encircle; shut (as a lid, door).

koopara: bellbird (*Anthornis melanura*).

koopare-a: veil, wreath; to shade, veil.

kooparu: bruised, crushed, mashed.

koopeke: cold.

koopenupenu: crush, mash.

koopeepee: pulpy, pulped.

koopeti: loop, noose.

koopikopiko: go to and fro, winding.

koo(pi)piri: contracted, shrivelled up, pinched with cold; crowded close together.

koopiro-a, -tia: duck, drench, immerse, soak, steep. **Kaanga koopiro:** fermented maize.

Koopuu: Venus (as morning star).

koopuu: abdomen, belly, womb.

kopuu: blistered.
koopua: deep pool.
koopuni: bunched together (of people moving).
koopura: seed kuumara.
kora: small fragment, spark, speck.
koraha: desert, moor, open country, wilderness.
koorahoraho: unfledged bird.
korakora: spark.
koorari: flower stalk of flax; flax (Northern dialect).
koorau: turnip.
kore: nothingness; a negativiser (LLM, 20.4). **Kaaore e kore:** without a doubt.
korekore: a phase of the waning moon.
koorekoreko: dazzled.
koorere: funnel, spout, tap.
koorero-tia: assert, declare, discuss, mention, read, say, talk, tell; fable, legend, news, message, saying, speech, tradition.
koorerorero: chatter, converse.
koretake: careless, useless.
korikori: bestir oneself, move about, wriggle.
korimako: bellbird (*Anthornis melanura*).
kooriparipa: dodge.
koro-a: desire.
koroheke: old (of people).
korohuu: steam.
koroiti: toe (little).
koroka, koroko: cloak.
korokee: fellow.
korokoro: slack; throat.

koromatua: thumb, toe (big).
koromaaungaunga: barnacle.
koromeke: crouch.
koronae: broadside on.
koroneihana: coronation.
koropaa: crowbar, crupper.
koropana: fillip.
koropiko: stoop, bow, make obeisance.
koropupuu: boil *v.*, bubble *v.*
kororaa: penguin, Little Blue.
koorori: twisted, of timber.
koorori-a: stir.
koorooria: glory.
korou-tia: desire; energy.
koroua-tia: old (of people), become old.
korowha: golf.
korowhiti: hoop, whistle.
koru: coil, loop.
koorua: pit.
korukoru: turkey, wrinkle.
koorupe: lintel.
koorure: change of wind.
kota: plane *v.*, shell (of bivalve).
kootaha: look sideways, sideways, sling.
kotahitanga: unity.
kootamutamu: smack the lips.
kootare: kingfisher (*Halcyon sanctus*).
kootero: potatoes steeped in water to ferment.
kooti: court *n.*; coach.
koti: coat.
kooti-a: reap.
kotiate: club (a type of).
kootimana: Scotch thistle.
kotinga: division, harvest.

kootingotingo: speckled.

kootiritiri: meteor.

kootiro: girl.

kootiti: dodge, wander, move aside.

kootiwhatiwha: freckled, spotted.

kotokoto: squeak.

kootore: backside, tail of certain birds.

kootua: turn the back.

kootui-a: interlace.

kootuku: white heron (*Egretta alba modesta*).

kootukutuku: native fuchsia (*Fuchsia excorticata*).

kooue: scull.

koukou: morepork, owl (*Ninox novaeseelandiae*); topknot.

kooura: crayfish.

koura: gold.

koowao: wild.

koowaawaa: neap tide.

kowee: scream.

koowhai: yellow; a tree (*Sophora* spp.).

koowhana: bend, bent.

koo(w)hanga: nest. **Koohanga reo:** Maori language kindergarten.

koowhao: hole, socket; leak.

koowhatu: monument, rock, stone.

ko(w)hera: start, twitch; yawn, gape.

kowheta: writhe, flounder about.

kowhetetia: scold.

koowhetewhete: scold.

koowhiri-a: pick, select; whirl.

koowhitiwhiti: grasshopper.

koowhiuwhiu: winnow, fan.

kua: content.

kuaha: door.

kuaka: godwit.

kuuao: young animal.

kuuare: foolish, ignorant, unaware.

kuha: gasp.

kuhakuha: ragged.

kuhu-a: enter, hide, be hidden, insert; put on (as clothes).

kuia: old woman.

kuihana: cushion.

kuiihi: goose; cushion; quince.

kuihipere: gooseberry.

kuiini: queen.

kuira: quilt.

kuki: cook *n.*

kuukuu: pigeon.

kuku: clamp *n.*, mussel, nightmare, pinchers, bivalve shellfish, vise.

kuku-a: close *v.*, haunt, nip; tweezers.

kukume (kuumea): drag, haul, pull, stretch, tow.

kuukupa: pigeon (Northern dialects).

kume: asthma.

kuumea: (*See* **kukume**).

kumete: bowl, trough.

kuumore: promontory.

kumu: posteriors, buttocks, backside.

kumukumu: gurnard (*Chelidonichthys kumu*).

kuupaa: belch.

kuupapa: stoop, remain
passive; a term applied to the
Maoris who fought with, or
did not fight against, the
settlers during the land wars.

kupenga: net, netting.

kuupere: gooseberry.

kupu: disobey, message,
saying, simile, speech,
word.

kura: school; red; valued
possesssion.

kuurae: headland, promontory.

kuurapa: vagabond.

kurii: dog, quadruped.

kuru: mallet.

kuru-a: beat, pound *v.*, rap,
thump.

kurupae: beam, joist.

kurupatu: hem (upper).

kuutai: mussel.

kutikuti: crop, shear, shears,
scissors.

kutu: louse. **Kutu papa:** crab
louse.

kuuwaha: entrance, gateway.

kuu(w)haa: thigh (especially
inner side of).

M

maa: clean, pale, pure, white.

ma(a): by way of (LLM,
18.33); and (LLM, 42.7); for
(LLM, 18.31).

mae: withered.

maea: gather (a crop); listless,
tired; at ease.

Maehe: March.

maaeneene: smooth.

maaero: mile.

maaha: gratified.

maha: frequent, many,
multitude, numerous,
plentiful.

maahaki: abate.

mahaki: meek, mild.

maahana: for him, for her
(Eastern dialect).

mahana: heat, warm.

maahanga: twins.

mahanga-tia: snare, noose.

mahara-tia: recollect, think;
thought.

maaharahara-tia: anxious;
anxiety, worry; think of,
take care of.

maahee: sinker.

mahi-a: work, toil, do,
perform; labour, action,
occupation, business. **Puku
mahi:** diligent, hard-
working.

mahinga: cultivation,
plantation.

maahita: master, teacher.

mahora: spread out.

mahore: peeled.

maahuu: gentle.

mahu: healed.

mahue: deserted, leave, be left.

maahunga: head.

mahura: uncover, uncovered.

maahuri: sapling.

mai: hither, this way, towards speaker (LLM, 21.1).

maaia: bold, brave, capable, courage, dare, resolute; fellow.

maiangi: floating, elevated.

maihea: sinker.

maihi: facing boards on gable of house, gable.

maikuku: claw, finger-nail.

maioro: embankment.

maitai: iron.

maaka: wild; mark.

maka-a: cast, fling, put aside, throw.

maakahi: wedge.

makariri: cold, winter.

makaroni: macaroni.

maakatikati: irritating.

makawe: hair of head, lock of hair.

makere: fall from a height, drop (as fruit from a tree).

maakete: auction, market.

maakona: satisfied, surfeited.

maakuu: damp, moist, wet.

maakuukuu: damp, moist.

makuru: fruitful.

maakutu: witch, wizard.

maakutu-ria: bewitch, witchcraft.

maamaa: light (weight).

mamae: ache, pain, sore, painful.

mamahi: assiduous, diligent, hard-working, industrious, toil.

mamaku: a tree-fern (*Cyathea medullaris*).

mamao: distant, distance.

mamaoa: vapour.

maminga-tia: crafty, deceive.

maamore: bare.

mana: authority, control, influence, power, prestige; effective.

manahau: cheerful.

manako-tia: like, want.

manatunga: keepsake.

manauri: sunburnt.

maanawa: mangrove (*Avicennia resinifera*).

manawa: belly, breath, heart.

manawa-nui: patient, stouthearted.

manawapaa: apprehensive, anxious.

manawa-tuu: cardiac arrest.

Mane: Monday.

maanene: importunate, asking again and again.

manene: wanderer.

maania: plain, flat land.

mania: slide, slip, slippery.

maniua: manure.

mano: host, many, multitude, thousand.

maanu: adrift, afloat, float, launched.

manu: bird; kite.

manuao: man-of-war, naval vessel.

manuhiri: guest, visitor.

maanuka: tea-tree (*Leptospermum* spp.).

maanukanuka: apprehensive, misgiving.

manumanu: collarbone.

mangaa: barracouta.

manga: bough, branch, brook.

maangai: mouth.

maangaro: good-tasting, as of mature kuumara, mealy.

maangere: idle, lazy, slothful.

maangiongio: chilblain.

mangoo: dogfish, shark.

mangu: black.

mangumangu: ink.

mangungu: closely woven.

maoa: cooked, ripe.

maaori: native, indigenous, ordinary.

maaota: green (of foliage).

maapere: marble.

mapi: diagram, map, plan.

maaporo: marbles (game).

maapu: flock of sheep, herd.

mapu: hum, pant, sigh, whizz.

maara: cultivated field, garden.

marae: courtyard in front of a meeting-house or at centre of a settlement.

marahihi: molasses. **Wai marahihi:** tobacco juice.

maarakerake: bare.

maarama: clear, evident, light (not dark), manifest, plain.

marama: month, moon.

maramara: bit, chip, fragment, morsel, piece, scrap, splinter.

maramataka: almanac, calendar.

maaramatanga: meaning, significance.

maranga: arise, rise up.

marangai: rain (Eastern dialects).

marara: dispersed, scattered; umbrella.

mare: cough, phlegm.

Mareia: Malaya.

maarena-tia: marry.

maarenatanga: marriage.

maarere: generous.

marere: fall, drop (as fruit from a tree); take off (of clothes).

marewa: raise, raised.

maarie: abate; appeased; quiet.

marino: calm (of sea).

maringi: spilt.

maripi: knife.

maarire: gentle, softly, thoroughly.

maariri: allayed, tranquillised; gentle, soft.

maaroo: fathom; hard, resolute, solid, stiff, tough, unyielding.

maro: apron, kilt.

maroke: dry.

maarooroo: strong.

maaroro: flying fish.

maruu: bruised, crush, crushed.

maru: shade, shelter, safeguard; power, authority.

marumaru: shade, sheltered from sun.

mataa: flint, lead, metal, obsidian.

mata: countenance, eye, face; green, unripe, raw, uncooked.

mataaho: window.

mataii: a tree (*Podocarpus spicatus*).

maatai: inspect, examine = **maataki(taki).**

maataitai: brackish. **Kai maataitai:** sea-food.

matakahi: wedge.

matakana: wary.

maataki(taki): see, watch, inspect, examine, gaze at, observe.

mata-kite: seer; vision.

matakookiri: meteor.

mataku: afraid, alarmed, dread, dreadful, fear, fright, frightened, terrible, timid.

matamata: extremity, point, tip.

maataamua: first-born.

maatanga: experienced.

matangerengere: cramped.

maatao: cold.

maataotao: cool.

matapihi: window.

matapoo: blind, a blind person.

matapoouri: gloomy.

maataapuna: source.

mataara: vigilant, awake. **Kai-mataara:** watchman.

matara: loose, undone, untie, untied.

matarau: spear with several points.

matarehi: mattress.

maataarere: forerunner.

Mata-riki: Pleiades, a star cluster whose heliacal rising in June marked the beginning of the year.

maatau: we all (but not you) (Eastern dialects).

matau: fish-hook; right (not left).

maatau-ria: adept, conscious, intelligent, know, skill, skilful, understand, wise.

maatauranga: knowledge, wisdom.

mate: dead, death, die; ill, sick, sickness, disease; beaten, defeated; misfortune, problem, defect.

mate-a: desire, want. **Mate taane:** lustful (of a woman). **Mate wahine:** lustful (of a man).

matekai: appetite, hunger.

mate-moe: sleepy.

maatene: mutton.

maatenga: head (Northern dialects).

maatere: lookout (on a ship).

mate-roto: abortion, miscarriage.

maatete: mustard.

mate-wai: thirst, thirsty.

maati: match.

matihe: sneeze.

matikara: toe.

maatikere: martingale.

maatiki: mattock.

matikuku: claw, finger-nail.

matimati: toe.

matire: fishing-rod.

matomato: green (of foliage).

maatotoru: thick.

maatou: us, we (but not you).

maatua: first; parents *pl.*

matua: aunt, father, mother, parent, uncle.

matuku: bittern, blue heron.

maaturuturu: drip, trickle.

maatuutuu: convalescent.

mau: confirmed, everlasting, fast, firm, fixed, made fast, imprisoned, seized.

mau-ria: carry, bring, lay hold of.

maaua: us, we two (but not you).

mauaahara: enmity, hate, malice.

mauii: left (not right).

maauiui: fatigued, sick, tired.

maauiuitanga: sickness, illness.

maaunu: bait.

maunu: withdrawn, loosened, taken off, come out.

maunga: mountain, ridge.

maauru: south-west.

mauru: appeased, eased (of pain), quieted.

mawehe: separated.

mawete: untie, untied.

maawhatu: curly, distinct curls.

maawhe: faded.

mawhera: open.

mawhiti: leap, skip; escape.

maawhitiwhiti: grasshopper, locust.

mea-tia: thing, object; do, say, think.

Mea: So-and-so, what's-his-name.

meake: soon.

meehua: measure.

Mei: May.

meiha: major; measure.

mekameka: chain.

meke-a: punch *v.*

mema: member.

memeha: pass away.

memene: (*See* **memenge**).

memenge: shrivelled, wither, withered, wrinkled.

    Memenge nga paapaaringa: smile.

menemana: amendment to a legal document.

mene(mene): assembled.

meneti: minute.

meera: mail.

merekara: miracle.

mere(mere): a short petal-shaped club of stone (especially greenstone).

mereni: melon.

merengi: melon.

meetara: metal.

miere: honey; powerless.

miihara: measles.

miiharo-tia: marvel, surprise, express wonder; admire.

mihi-a: admire, greet, lament.

mihinare: missionary.

miihini, mihiini: machine, machine saw.

Mihingare: Anglican.

mimi (miia): urine, urinate.

mimiti: absorbed; evaporate; low (of tide); vanished (of people).

minamina: desire, wish.

minita: minister.

mira: looking-glass, mirror; mill.

miraka-tia: milk.

miri-a: rub.

mirimiri: fondle.

mirione: million.

miro: a tree (*Podocarpus ferrugineus*).

miro-a: string, thread, spin thread, twist strands into a thread or cord.

miitara: measles.

miiti: meat. **Miiti poaka:** pork.

miti(miti)-a: lick.

mo(o): because, concerning, for, about, on account of (LLM, 17).

moana: ocean, open sea.

moata: early; mortar.

moe-a: asleep, sleep; sleep with, have sex, marry. **Moe taane, moe wahine:** marriage.

moemoeaa: dream.

moenga: bed.

moeroa: sleepyhead.

moohio-tia: know, believe that one knows, comprehend, understand; adept, intelligent, skilful, wise; knowledge, skill.

moho: blockhead.

mohoao: barbarian, barbarous.

moohuu: selfish.

mohu: smoulder.

moimoi: call a dog.

mooiri: suspend, suspended.

mookai: servant, slave; pet animal or bird.

mokemoke: lonely, solitary.

mookete-tia: mortgage.

mooki(h)i: raft made of flax stalks or raupoo.

moko: tattoo (especially facial).

moko(moko): lizard, skink.

mokopuna: grandchild.

mokowhiti: beat, palpitate; pulse.

momi-a: suck.

momo: breed, kind.

momoe: drowsy, sleepy.

moomona: fatty (of meat, fish); be fat, obese.

momoto (motokia): strike with fist, box.

momotu (motuhia): snap, break (as a stick, bone), severed.

moonenehu: cover with spray; dimly seen, indistinct.

moni: money. **Moni maaka:** deposit.

mono-kia: caulk.

mongamonga: crush, crushed.

more: headland; tap-root.

moorehu: survivor.

moremore: bare.

moorere: swing.

moorikarika: vexed, troubled; disgusted.

morimori: branchless.

mooro: maul *n.*

mooteatea: faint-hearted.

mootini: motion, resolution.

motokaa: automobile, car, motor-car.

motokia: (*See* momoto).

motu: island; clump or grove of trees; severed (*See* momotu).

motuhake: separate, distinct. **Mana motuhake:** separate identity and authority.

motuhia: (*See* momotu).

motupaika: motor bike.

moua: mower.

moumou: waste.

moounu: bait = **maaunu.**

moutere: island.

moowhiti: hoop, ring; spectacles.

muu: draughts (game).

mua: ahead, before, former, formerly, front, the past.

muhukai: inattentive.

mui(mui)-a: beset, cluster, swarm over (as flies).

muku(muku)-a: wipe.

mumura, mura(mura): blaze, flame; glow, be brilliantly coloured, blush.

muri: after, afterwards, behind, rear; breeze; future.

muurihi: muesli.

muri-tai: sea breeze.

muriwai: backwater.

muru-a: plunder, strip (as leaves from a tree); wipe, wipe off; forgive; smear on.

mutu: cease, cut, ended, finished, ceased.

mutumutu-a: crop, cut short.

mutunga: conclusion, consequence, end, termination.

mutunga-kore: endless, eternal.

N

Note: Words beginning with NG are listed separately.

na!: behold!, now then!

naa: gratified, satisfied.

na(a): possessive marker (LLM, 17, 18.); there (near person spoken to) (LLM, 3, 15.1). **Na reira, no reira:** therefore (LLM, 18.23).

naenae: gnat, mosquito.

naeroa: gnat, mosquito.

naahea: when?

naahi, neehi: nurse *n.*

Naahinara: National (party).

naaianei: immediately, today, now. Usually prefixed by **o-, no-, i-.**

naihi: knife.

naakahi: serpent, snake.

naaku: mine, belonging to me.

nama: debt, number.

namata: formerly.

namu: fly, sandfly.

nana: behold.

nanahi: yesterday.

nanakia: fierce.

nanao, naomia: handle *v.*, lay hold of.

nanati (naatia), nati(nati): constrict, choke.

nanekoti: nanny-goat.

nanenane: goat.

nanu: mixed.

naonao: midge.

napikena: napkin.

naatia: (*See* **nanati**).

nati(nati): (*See* **nanati**).

nawe: scar *n.*

neehi: nurse *n.*

nehu: dust.

nei: here, this. Marks position near speaker (LLM, 3., 15.1). Used in relative clauses (LLM, 49.2).

neinei: a tree (*Dracophyllum latifolium*).

neke: snake.

neke-hia: move, shift; roller.

nekeneke-hia: move about.

neketai: necktie.

nenewha: close eyes, doze.

neera: nail *n.*

niao: gunwale.

niho: tooth, tusk; bit (drill). **Niho puu:** molar tooth.

ninihi: slink, stealthily go.

no(o): from, belonging to. Mark of subordinate possession (LLM, 18.21). **No reira:** therefore, accordingly.

noa: unrestricted, non-tapu, common, ordinary, random. Particle marking lack of restriction or definition (LLM, 22.4). **Noa iho:** only, just, quite.

noatia: passive form of particle **noa**.

Noema: November.

nohinohi: little, small.

noho-ia: sit; abide, cohabit, dwell, inhabit, live, remain, stay.

nohoanga: seat, dwelling place, saddle.

noho-puku: silent, be.

nooku: mine (LLM, 18.4).

noni: bend, bent, crooked.

nonoti (nootia): constrict, pinch, strangle, suffocate.

nootia: (*See* **nonoti**).

Nuu Ia: New Year.

nui: big, large, great, famous, many, abundant, abundance. **Ka nui teenaa:** that is enough. **Nui haere:** increase.

nuinga: extent, size.

nukarau-tia: deceive.

nuke(nuke): crooked.

nuku: earth as opposed to sky (**rangi**).

nuku(nuku)-hia: move, shift.

nunui: big (*pl.* form of **nui**).

nunumi: disappear, disappeared, pass behind.

nuupepa: newspaper.

NG

nga(a): the (*pl.* definite article) (LLM, 2.2).

ngaa: satisfied, appeased (of an appetite or emotion).

Whakangaa: take breath, breathe.

ngaehe: rustle.

ngahae: tear, torn.

ngahau: cheerful, hearty; entertainment.

ngahengahe: forest.

ngahere: forest, bush.

ngaaherehere: forest, bush.

ngaahoahoa: headache.

ngahuru: autumn, harvest.

ngaakahi: serpent.

ngaakau: bowels, entrails; heart (seat of emotions).

ngaakau-kore: disinclination.

ngaakau-nui: eager.

ngaki-a: cultivate, dig, weed; avenge, revenge.

ngako: fat *n*.

ngangaa: cry loudly, bawl.

nganga: hail *n*.

ngangahu: make faces, distort face as in performing the war-dance.

ngangare: dispute.

ngangau: disturbance.

ngaoki: crawl, creep.

ngaoko: itch, tickle.

ngapu: quake.

ngaarara: insect, grub, reptile.

ngare-a: order, send, urge.

ngaarehu: embers.

ngaro: out of sight, absent, destroyed, disappear, disappeared, hidden, lost, missing.

ngaru: wave *n*.

ngarue: shake.

ngarungaru: rough (of the sea).

ngaaruru: surfeited.

ngata: satisfied; slug, snail.

ngaatahi: together.

ngatari: vibrate.

ngaatata: chapped, chasm, cracked.

ngau-a: bite, chew, gnaw.

ngaaueue: oscillate, shake.

ngaawari: easy, flexible, mild, obedient, soft, supple, tender.

ngawii: howl, scream, squeal.

ngawingawi: whine, whinge, cry (of a baby or child).

ngaawhaa: hot spring.

ngawhaa: burst forth; come into bloom. **Poho ngawhaa:** heartburn.

ngawhara: crumbled.

ngaawhaariki: brimstone; sulphur.

ngawhewhe: worn-out, torn (as of clothes).

ngehengehe: flabby.

ngene: wrinkled, full of folds; a wen.

ngenge: fatigued, tired, exhaustion, weariness.

ngeengere: purr (of a cat).

ngerengere: leprosy (so called). It is unlikely that true leprosy was present in New Zealand in early times.

ngeru: cat.

ngerungeru: sleek, smooth.

ngingio: shrivelled, wrinkled.

ngio: extinguished, gone out.

ngira: needle.

ngohengohe: flabby, flexible, pliable, soft, supple, tender.

ngohi: fish.

ngoi: energy, strength; crawl, creep.

ngira: needle.
ngohengohe: flabby, flexible, pliable, soft, supple, tender.
ngohi: fish.
ngoi: energy, strength; crawl, creep.
ngoikore: feeble, languid, listless, powerless, weak.
ngoingoi: creep, crawl.
ngooiro: conger eel, sea eel.
ngooki: crawl, creep.

ngongore: blunt. **Matau ngongore:** a hook without a barb.
ngongoro: snore.
ngote-a: suck.
nguu: dumb, speechless; squid (*Sepia apama*).
nguha: rage, raging.
nguunguu: mutter.
ngunguru: grunt, murmur, rumble.
ngutu: lip, beak, bill.

O

oo: food for a journey, provisions.
o: preposition marking subordinate possession, of (LLM, 13.1–4).
oati: promise.
oha: generous, liberal.
oohaakii: parting or dying wish or pronouncement, will (legal).
oho: awake, wake, sudden start.
ohorere: alarmed.
ohu: band of people, working party, working bee.
oioi: shake.
oka-ina: butcher-knife, dagger; prick, stab, stick.
oke-a: struggle.
okeoke: restless, wriggle, writhe.
Oketopa: October.

ookiha: ox.
okioki: pause, rest.
oko: trough, bowl.
ooku: my (*pl.* possession) (LLM, 14.1–2).
oma-kia: run, runner, run after.
one: beach.
oneone: earth, dirt, ground, soil.
onepuu: sand.
ono: six.
ono-kia: to plant.
ongaonga: nettle (*Urtica* spp.).
ope: army, band, company, party, group, troop.
oopure: pied, varied in colour.
ora: alive; cured; escaped, survived; fit and well, healthy; fed; wedge (for splitting timber); slave.

oranga: comfort, consolation, food, health, safety, salvation.

ore-a: to bore, probe.

oreore: move about.

oriwa: olive.

oro: grove of trees of one kind; echo, rumble.

oro-hia: grind on a stone.

Ooropi: Europe.

oru: boggy.

oruoru: few.

oota: order.

ota-ina: green of fruit, uncooked, unripe; eat raw.

otaota: herbs, rubbish, weeds.

ooti: oats.

oti: accomplish, accomplished, complete, be complete, finished, completed. **Haere oti atu:** go for good.

otinga: conclusion, end.

otita: auditor (commercial).

Ooturu: full moon.

ouou: few.

oowhanga: nest.

P

paa: fortress; weir to trap eels; shelter-belt of trees; barricade; spinner (fish-hook); be hit (as by a stone). **Paa-tuuwatawata:** fort with stockade.

Paa: term of address to older or superior male, sir.

paa-ia: block up, obstruct, dam.

paa-kia: strike, slap, hit.

paa-ngia: smite (as illness, disease); blow (as wind).

pae: perch, ridge, any transversely placed obstacle. **Pae o te rangi:** horizon.

pae-a: cast on shore, surround, wrecked.

paemanu: collarbone.

paenga: site.

paepae: threshold of a house; the beam of a traditional latrine; the host speakers at a ceremonial gathering.

paaera-tia: boil, boiler.

paerata: pilot.

paahau: beard.

pahemo: miss, pass by.

paahi: boss, employer; purse, wallet.

pahii: encampment.

pahi: bus.

paahihi: passenger.

paahikete-pooro: basketball.

paahiwihiwi: uneven (of a surface).

paaho: broadcast.

paahoahoa: headache.

pahuu: explode, burst.

paahua-tia: rob.

pahure: escaped, passed by.

pai: good, advantage.
pai-ngia: to like, approve; consent.
paiaka: root.
paihamu: opossum.
paihau: wing; fin of flying fish or gurnard; beard.
paiheneti: per cent.
paihere-tia: tie in bundles; bundle.
paihikara: bicycle.
paihini: poison.
paikaraaihe-tia: binoculars, telescope; spy on, surveillance.
paina: pine tree.
painaaporo: pineapple.
pai-oneone: clod.
paipa: pipe, tobacco. **Kai paipa:** smoke tobacco.
paipera: Bible.
pairi: disquieted.
paaka: box.
paka: dried, baked; scab; bugger!
pakapaka: pork crackling.
paakaakaa: brown.
pakakee: whale.
pakanga-tia: battle, hostilities, quarrel, war.
pakari: hard, mature, strong.
pakaru: broken, smashed, torn, wrecked.
paakaru(karu)-tia, -a: break, smash, break through.
paakau: kite, wing.
pakau: fracture, fractured.
paakauroharoha: grasshopper.
paakau-rua: sting-ray.
paakawe-tia: shoulder *v.*

Paakehaa: white (person).
pakeke: adult; age; hard, solid, stiff.
paakete: bucket; pocket-knife; pocket; handkerchief.
paki: fair weather, fine weather; buggy.
pakiaka: root.
pakihawa: clumsy; throat fin.
pakihiwi: shoulder.
pakini: nip, pinch.
pakipaki: clap, pat.
paakira: bald.
pakitara: gossip, wall.
paakiwaha: boast.
pakiwaitara: fable.
pakiwhara: naked; venereal disease.
pakoo: pop.
paakohu: chasm, gully; rent, cleft.
paakoro: storehouse.
pakuu: resound.
paku: scab.
pakupaku: little, small.
paakura: swamp hen (*Porphyrio porphyrio*) = **puukeko.**
paakuru: knock.
paamamao: distant, distance.
paamu: farm.
pana-a: banish, expel, push.
pana-a: eject.
panana: banana.
paananaki: gentle slope.
panapana: beat (of heart), throb.
pane: head.
panekoti: petticoat, slip.
pani: orphan.

pani-a: besmear, daub, paint, smear.

panihi: punch, blow with fist.

panikena: pannikin.

Paaniora: Spaniard.

paanui-tia: publish, advertise, make known.

paanuku: sledge.

panga-a, -ia: cast, throw.

panga: riddle.

pango: black.

pao-a: crack, cracked, pound, smash, smashed, strike; hatch.

paoa: smoke.

paoi: beater, pestle.

paaoka: fork.

paaoro: ball.

paaoro-tia: resound, echo; jarred by harsh sounds.

paoro: echo, resound, reverberate.

paapaa: father.

papaa: explode.

papa: board, plank, slab; a flat place; ground of quarrel, etc.; mesh of a net; buttocks. **Papa kaainga:** village ground, reserve.

paapaka: crab.

papaki (paakia): rap, slap.

paapaki: patch.

paapaku: low, shallow.

papanga: site.

paapapa: bran, chaff.

paapara: poplar.

paaparakaauta: hotel, public house.

papare (parea): ward off, parry.

paapaaringa: cheek, smile.

paparua: double.

papatahi: flat.

papatairite: level, flat.

papatua: uncultivated (of land).

papi: puppy, pup.

paapura: purple.

para: pollen, sediment.

parae: plain, flat and uncultivated area.

paaraharaha: flat (not round).

paraahi: brass; brush, toothbrush.

parai: fry.

paraihe: award, prize; brass; brush.

paraikete: blanket.

paraina: blind (screen).

Paraire: Friday.

paraire: bridle.

parakete: booty, plunder.

parakimete: blacksmith.

parakitihi-tia: practise, practice.

parakuihi: breakfast.

paramu: plum; plumb-line.

paramureta: perambulator, pram.

parana: verandah.

paranene: flannel.

parani-tia: brand; brandy.

paraaoa: bread, flour; sperm-whale, whale.

paraaone: brown.

parapara: garbage, rubbish; filth; offal; spittle; a part of the afterbirth.

pararaiha: paralyse, paralysis.

parararaki: shallow (of a dish).

pararee: bawl, shout.

parareka: potato.
pararuutiki: paralytic.
paratiki: plastic.
parau: falsehood, lie; plough.
parauri: dark.
paare, paarei: barley.
pare: garland, peak of a cap, wreath.
pare-a: band, headband, bodice; to band.
paarei: barley.
parekura: battle in which many are killed, battle-field, victims killed in battle, slaughter.
parekura: fight.
paaremata: parliament.
paaremete: parliament.
paaremoremo: slippery.
pare-nga: bank of river.
parengo: slip.
paarengorengo: slippery.
parepare: breastwork.
pa(a)rera: duck (*Anas* spp.). Ngutu parera: flintlock musket.
paareti: porridge.
pari: cliff, echo, precipice, tide, flood.
paariiraatanga: intermission.
parirau: wing.
paaroo: palm of hand; small basket of or for cooked food.
paarore: relaxing, relaxed.
parore: shitfish (*Girella tricuspidata*), now sold as Pacific Supreme.
parori: awry, crooked.
paarua: brim.

paru(paru): earth, dirt, filth, mud, dirty, muddy, soiled.
paarurenga: booty.
paata: pot.
pata: drop (of liquid); butter.
paatai-a, -ngia: ask, question, enquire, inquire, query.
paataka: storehouse.
paatara: bottle.
paataritari: entice.
paatata: close near, near.
patatee: make cracking or popping sound.
paatene: batten; button.
paatere: chant, flow.
paati: patch; party; perch (unit of area); barge.
patii: spurt.
paatiki: field, paddock; various species of flatfish, flounder, sole.
pati(pati): beg, coax.
paatiitii: grass; hatchet.
patoo-hia: crack, cracked.
paatohe: fallow.
paatootoo: knock.
paatuu: wall.
patu-a: beat, club, kill, slaughter, strike; club, weapons in general.
paatukituki: knock.
patunga: sacrifice.
patupatu: beat (of heart).
pau: consume, consumed, exhausted, expended, finished, all gone, spent.
paukena: pumpkin.
pauna-tia: pound (money or weight); weigh, weight; steelyard, swingle-tree.

paura: powder (including blasting-, gun-); smut in wheat. **Peekana-paura:** baking-powder.

paawera: apprehensive; heat.

paa-whakarua: north-east wind.

paawhara-tia: cut, rip.

pee: crush, crushed; roe.

pea: perhaps.

peha: bark, husk, peel, rind, skin.

peehea-tia: like how?

peehi-a: press upon, suppress; forbid.

pehipehi: sill.

pehipehia: ambush.

pei: spade.

pei-a: banish, eject, expel.

peihana: basin; pheasant.

peipei: jostle.

peeita: paint.

peka-ina: bough, branch; firewood; go aside, turn aside.

peekana: bacon.

pekanga: crossroad, fork of a tree, branch path.

pekapeka: bat (animal).

peeke: bag, sack; bank (financial).

peke: foreleg, jump, leap.

pekepeke: hop of a bird.

pekii: chirp.

peenaa-tia: like that.

peena: pan.

peene: band (musical).

pene: pen, pencil. **Pene raakau:** pencil.

pene waiwaha: ink pencil.

penehiini: benzine, gasoline, petrol.

peenei-tia: like this, thus; do like this.

peeneti: bayonet.

penetiini: benzine, gasoline, petrol.

penihana: pension.

penu: mash.

penupenu: mashed.

pepa: paper, form; pepper.

peepee: pulpy, pulped.

pepeha: witticism.

peepeke: bend of knees.

peepepe: butterfly.

peepi: baby.

Pepuere: February.

peeraa-tia: like that; do like that.

peera: bail, bale.

pera: pillow.

peere: bucket, pail; bail; bale.

pere: bell.

pere-a: cast a dart; dart.

perehi-tia: printing press; print, publish.

Perehipitiiriana: Presbyterian.

perehitini: president.

pereki: brick; brig; brake.

peereni: paling.

pereti, pureti: plate.

perohuuka: bill-hook.

peru: head of a nail.

peruperu: wattles of a bird; a kind of potato.

peeti: bed; mattock; spade (suit in cards).

peto: consume, consumed.

pewa: eyebrow. **Pewa ika:** roe of a fish.

121

peewara: bevel.

pee(w)hea-tia: how; treat in what fashion.

pii: bee; chicken, young bird; pea.

pia: beer; sap.

piana: piano.

piiata(ata): bright, shining, shine.

piha: butcher shop; gill.

piharau: lamprey.

piha-reinga: cricket (insect).

piihi: piece.

piihikete: biscuit.

pihi(pihi): sprout.

pihipihi: wax-eye (*Zosterops lateralis*).

piihoihoi: ground-lark (*Anthus novaeseelandiae*).

piihopa: bishop. **Piihopatanga:** diocese.

piihuka: fish-hook, hook.

piikake: peacock.

piikaokao: fowl, hen.

piikara: pickle.

piikau-tia: carry on the back.

piki: feathers, plumes; fig.

piki-arero: palate; clematis (*Clematis* spp.).

pikiniki: picnic.

piki-tia: ascend, climb.

pikitanga: ascent.

pikitia: film movie, picture.

piko: bend, bent, stoop.

Pikopoo: Roman Catholic.

pine-a: pin.

piini: bean.

piinohi-tia: tongs, use tongs.

piingao: a shore grass used in weaving (*Desmoschoenus spiralis*).

piingore: flexible.

piioi-tia: brandish.

piopio: thrush.

pipii: ooze.

pipi: various edible bivalve species.

piipipi: turkey.

piipiiwharauroa: shining cuckoo (*Chalcites lucidus lucidus*).

piira: appeal (legal).

piirairaka: fantail (*Rhipidura flabellifera*).

piirangi-tia: crave, desire, like *v.*, want, wish.

pirau: decayed, putrid, rotten; pus, matter; extinguished.

pire: account, bill (financial or political).

piri: stick to, adhere, cling; skulk.

pirihi: priest.

pirihimana: policeman, constable.

pirihoo: fleece, fleece-o.

pirimia: premier.

piriniha: prince.

pirinitete: princess.

piringa: refuge.

piriota, piriote: billiards.

piripiri: curly, woolly, woolly of hair; burr, bidibid.

piriti: bridge.

piriwheke: prefect.

piro: bad, fetid, odour, stench, stink.

pita: bit for horse.

piitara: pistol.

piiti: beaten, defeated.

piititi: peach.

pito: end, extremity, navel.

piitoitoi: robin (*Petroica australis*).

piu-a: sling, toss.

piukara, piukera: bugle.

piupiu-a: wave about, move to and fro, oscillate; dance skirt.

piuta: solder.

pi(i)wa: fever.

piiwaiwaka: fantail (*Rhipidura* spp.).

piiwakawaka: fantail (*Rhipidura* spp.).

poo: darkness, night. **Te Poo:** the spirit world of the dead.

poo-ngia: benighted, overtaken by darkness.

poai: boy.

poaka: pig. **Miiti poaka:** pork.

poapoa: bait, entice.

poari: board (committee). **Kooti poari:** board of enquiry.

pooauau: bewildered, confused, mistaken.

poohauhau: stupid.

pohe: (*See* po(po)he).

pooheehee: confuse, confused, mistaken, deluded.

pohewa: deluded.

poohi: post; boss, employer.

pohi: boss, employer.

poohimaahita: postmaster.

poho: breast, bosom.

poohue: several climbing plants, bindweed, convolvulus.

poohuuhuu: cluster.

poohutuhutu: splash, splashed.

pohutukawa: Christmas tree.

poihaa: butcher-shop (Taranaki dialect).

poi(poi)-a: a padded ball of flax, raupoo, corn-husk, etc., on a string; twirl, swing, wave about; make into a ball, knead.

pooito: net float.

poka-ia, -ina: grave, hole; pierce; operate on surgically; castrate.

pookai-a: wind into a ball or coil; flock of birds. **Pookai whenua:** travel about.

pokapoka: docking knife; scrofula.

poke: soiled, dirty, stained.

poke-a: haunt.

pokepoke: knead or mix with liquid.

pookia: (*See* popoki).

poko: extinguished.

pokohiwi: shoulder *n*.

pokorua: pit, hollow.

pona-ia: joint (ankle, elbow); knot (in wood), knuckle; tie.

poonitanita: thistle, Scotch thistle.

pono: befall; faithful, true, truth.

pononga: servant.

ponga: a tree-fern (*Cyathea dealbata*).

pongaihu: nostril.

pongaponga: nostril.

poopoo: knead.

popoo: crowd round, throng.

po(po)he, (poohea): wither, withered (of leaves); dull, stupid; dead, death; blind, blinded.

popoki, (pookia): overrun.

poopokorua: ant.

popono: covet.

popoto: short.

poraka: block (of land); frog; frock, jersey, pullover.

poorangi-tia: beside oneself, hasty, hurry, idiot, impatient, insane, mad, crazy, delirious.

pooraruraru: confused, confounded.

poorearea: tiresome.

porera: floor mat.

pooringi-hauihi: boarding-house.

pooriro: bastard.

pooro: ball.

poro: block of wood, log; butt.

poro-a: broken, crop, cut.

poroka: frog.

poropeihana: probation.

poropiti: prophet.

poorori: bastard.

porotaka: round.

porotiti: roll, turn, revolve, twirl; disc.

poro(w)hita: round.

poorutu: splash, splashed.

pootae-a: cap, hat; surround.

pootaka: top (whipping).

pootatu: hurry.

pooti-tia: election, vote.

poti: boat; cat.

Pootikii: Portuguese.

pooturi: slow.

pou-a: post.

pouahi: bellows.

pouaka: box *n*. **Pouaka aihi:** freezer. **Pouaka maatao:** refrigerator. **Pouaka whakaata:** television.

pouaru: widow.

pounamu: greenstone, jade; bottle.

poupou: perpendicular, steep; stake.

poupoutanga o te raa: noon.

pourewa: stage.

poouri: dark, distress, distressed, grief, mournful, sad, sorrow, sorrowful.

poouriuri: gloomy.

poutaapeta: post office.

pouto: float *n*.

pouturi: stubborn.

poowhatu: rock, stone.

poowhiri-tia: beckon, greet, wave, welcome.

puu: gun; heap, heaped up; source. **Puu ahi:** cigarette lighter.

pua: blossom.

puaka: dry twigs, brush (especially tea-tree).

puapua: shield.

puare: exposed, open.

puuaaritarita: hurry.

puuaawai-tia: blossom, flower, to flower; come to fruition (of a project).

puuawhe-a: backed (of sails).

puehu: dust.

puuhaa: sow-thistle.

puha: gill (of fish); butcher-knife.

puuhaehae: envious, jealous, jealousy.

puuhahana: hot to the taste, inflamed.

puuhana: glow.

puuhera: bushel.

puhi: virgin; plume.

puuhia: (*See* **pupuhi**).

puhipuhi: tuft; bunched up (as of hair).

puhuki: blunt.

puuhuruhuru: hairy.

puia: steam.

puihi: bush, forest.

puukahukahu: spongy.

puukai-tia: heap, heaped up, heap up.

pukapuka: book, letter, document; lungs.

puke: hill.

puukeko: swamp hen (*Porphyrio porphyrio*).

puukenga: source or repository of knowledge.

pukepuke: mound.

puukiki: stunted.

puukohu: fog.

puu-koorero: orator.

puukoro: sheath; condom.

puukoru: fold *n.*

puku: abdomen, abscess, belly, intestines, tumour; knob, knot in wood; swell; secretly.

puku-kai: greedy.

puku-mahi: assiduous, hard-working, industrious.

puku-nui: glutton, gluttony.

puku-paa: barren (of woman).

puku-riri: angry, cross, furious, surly; anger, wrath.

puumahu: steamy.

puumau: constant.

puna: spring of water, well-water.

pune: spoon.

puunehunehu: misty.

puni: blocked up, encampment, stopped, blocked.

puunu: spoon.

punua: young animal.

punuki: blunt.

punga-a: anchor.

pungapunga: pumice; yellow.

pungarehu: ashes.

puungaawerewere: cobweb, spider.

puupaa: belch.

puupuu: various kinds of univalve molluscs, especially *Lunella smaragda* and *Zediloma aethiops*.

pupuu: to bubble, boil, well up.

pupuhi, (puuhia): blow; shoot (gun), fire.

pupuri, (puritia): stop, restrain, hold back, cling to, detain, hold, keep.

pupuru, (purutia): stop, restrain, hold back, cling to, detain, hold, keep.

puurakau: legend, myth, fable. Usually **Koorero puuraakau**.

puramu: plum.

puuranga-tia: heap, heaped up, heap up.

purapura: seed, including tubers retained as seed-stock.

puuraatoke: glow-worm.

purei-tia: play. **Purei hooiho:** horse race.

puurekereke: puff of wind.

puuremu-tia: adultery, commit adultery.

puurena: brimful, overflow.

purepure: pied, tufted, spotted.

puurerehua: moth.

puurero: project, show (above surface of water).

pureti: plate. **Pureti niho:** denture.

purini, puringi: pudding. **Puringi korikori:** jelly.

puritanga: handle, knob, door-knob.

puri-tia: (*See* **pupuri**).

puurotu: agreeable.

p(u)uru: bull.

puruu: blue.

puru: plug, bung, cork.

puurua: pair.

puruhi: flea.

purukamu: blue-gum.

puruuma: broom.

puruuma-tia: sweep.

puru(puru)-a: cork, plug, block up, stop, stuff up; put into.

puta: anus; appear, emerge, escape, succeed, pass through and out; hole, nostril, opening, pass through. **Puta noa:** throughout. **Niho puta:** tusk.

puutahi: join, meet (as paths, streams).

puutake: base, cause, reason, origin.

puutanetane: retch.

putanga: passage, way of escape, way out, exit.

puutangitangi: paradise duck (*Tadorna variegata*).

puutara(tara), puu-taatara: trumpet made from univalve volute shells.

puutawa: fungus that was dried and used as tinder.

puutea: bag. **Puutea moni:** fund.

puutia: butcher, butcher-knife.

putiputi: flower.

puutoi: bunch.

puutongatonga-marangai: south-east.

puutorino: flute.

puutoto: bloody.

puutu: boot, foot measure.

putuputu: frequent.

puuwhaa: sow thistle (*Sonchus* spp.) widely used as greens.

puuwhero: reddish.

R

raa: sail *n*. **Raa-ngongohau:** jib sail.

raa: day; sun. **Raa horoi:** Saturday. **Raa tapu:** Sunday.

rae: forehead; headland, promontory.

rahi: big, great, large; size.

rahirahi: thin. **Taringa rahirahi:** touchy, quick to take offence.

raho: testicle.

raho(raho)-a: floor, deck, floorboards.

rahu-a: foiled, be.

raahui-tia: conserve a resource by placing a ban on its use, ban; reserve.

rahurahu: meddle with, interfere, handle; brackenfern (*Pteridium esculentum*).

raihana: licence.

raaihe: enclosure. **Raaihe poaka:** sty.

raihi: rice.

raima: cement, lime.

raaina: boundary, line fishing.

raiona: lion.

raiti: lamp, light.

raiwhara: rifle.

raka: adept, skilful.

rakaraka: harrow.

raka-tia: lock.

raakau: stick, plant, tree, wood, timber; weapon.

raakau-nui: full moon.

raakei-tia: adorn, embellish.

raakete: racquet.

raki: north.

rakiraki: duck (domestic).

rakuraku: rake; scratch.

rama: light, lamp, torch.

ranea: copious.

raanei: mark of interrogation.

raanei . . . raanei: either . . . or.

ranu-a: mix.

ranga: shoal, school (of fish).

ranga-a: raise, pull up; avenge a death.

rangatira: boss, chief; ennoble; chiefly.

rangi: day; heaven, sky; tune, air. **Taha atu o te rangi:** horizon.

rangimaarie: peace and quiet, lack of conflict.

rangirangi-a: vex, vexed.

rangirua: uncertain.

rango: house-fly; roller or skid for moving heavy objects.

rangona: heard. (*See* **rongo-hia**).

raaoa: choked.

raorao: plain *n.*

rapa-ngia: adhere, stick to; seek, look for.

raapeti: rabbit.

raapihi: rubbish.

raapoi-tia, -a: assemble, gather together, cluster, swarm.

rapu-a: look for, search, seek.

rapurapu: doubt, doubtful.

rara-a: toast or grill (especially fish).

rara: rib.

raranga (rangaa): plait (as baskets, floor-mats) from flax etc. by the technique often called weaving.

raarangi: line of print, row, line.

ra(ra)pa: flash, sparkle.

ra(ra)pi-hia, rapirapi: scratch.

ra(ra)ta: tame, quiet (of a horse).

rarau: handle *v.*

rarauhe: bracken-fern (*Pteridium esculentum*).

ra(ra)whi-a: grasp, seize, hold firmly.

rare: lolly.

raro: below, bottom; north wind, north.

raru: troubled, perplexed, vexed, busy; problem, trouble, business.

raruraru: trouble; business, matters needing attention.

rata: doctor; quiet, tame, domesticated.

raatana: lamp, lantern.

raati: harpoon, lance.

rato: serve, be served of food.

raatou: they.

rau: hundred; leaf, blade (of club).

raaua: they (two), them (two) (LLM, 9.3).

raumati: summer.

raupaa: chapped, calloused.

raupani: frying-pan.

raupeka: doubt, doubtful.

raupoo: bulrush (*Scirpus* spp.).

rauriki: sow-thistle (*Sonchus* spp.) eaten as greens.

rau(w)iri-tia: intertwine.

rawa: goods, property; particle marking intensity or immediacy (LLM, 22.1), very. **Tangata whai rawa:** well-to-do person.

raawaho: outsider.

rawakore: poor, destitute.

rawe: adept, able; excellent, suitable.

raweke-tia: meddle, molest, tamper with; manipulate, fashion.

raawhara: raffle.

raawhiti: east. **Tai raawhiti:** east coast.

rehe-a: baffled, balked.

reehita-tia: register. **Kai-reehita:** registrar.

rehu-a: haze, mist, spray; indistinctly (seen); a vision.

rehutai: spray.

rei: ivory, precious ornament of ivory.

rei puta: tusk.

reimana: layman.

reina: reins.

Reipa: Labour (party).

reira: that aforementioned place. **Na reira, no reira:** therefore.

reiri: lady.

reiti: rates (tax).

reka: flavour *n.*, nice, palatable, pleased, sweet.

rekareka: delighted, be, itch, pleasant, tickle *n.*

reekena: leggings.

rekereke: heel.

rekureihana: regulation.

reemana: lemon.

reme: lamb.

remu: border of garment, hem (lower), tail of bird; yeast used in leavened bread.

reo: language, speech, voice.

repo: bog, marsh, swamp; cannon.

reera: rail (of fence).

rera: leather, strap.

rere: fly (of a bird), flow (of water), carried off (on the wind), sail (of a boat), throw oneself from a height, leap; flee, escape; cataract, waterfall.

rere-ngia: leap.

rererangi: aeroplane, plane, aircraft.

rererua: double.

reerewee, reeriwee: railway.

reri: ready.

reta: letter.

reeti: let, lease, rent.

reetuu: lay to (of a vessel).

rewa: float, afloat, launched (of a boat); melt (of fat, etc.); raised on high.

reewara: level (tool).

reewera: devil.

rewha: eyelid, squint.

rewharewha: cold, influenza.

rewherii-tia: referee.

riha: nit.

rihariha: disgusting.

riihi-tia: dish, plate; lease.

riihiiti: receipt.

rika: sapling kauri.

rikarika: annoyed, be.

riiki: leek; league.

rikiriki: fragment.

riikona: deacon.

rikoriko: twinkle.

rima: five.

rimu: red pine (*Dacrydium cupressinum*); seaweed; moss.

rimurimu: moss, seaweed.

riinena: linen.

rino: iron; lock of hair.

ringaringa: hand and arm, hand, arm; weapon (figuratively).

ringa wera: cooks and kitchen-hands.

riingi: ring.

riingi-hia: call on the telephone.

riipeka-tia: cross *n.*, crucify; passion-fruit. **Ara riipeka:** crossroads.

riipene, riipine: ribbon; audio tape.

riipenetaa: repent.

ripi-a: cut, slash.

ripo: eddy; the stretch of calm water between rapids on a river.

riipoata: report.

riporipo: curl of smoke, whirlpool.

rirerire: cricket (insect).

riri (riiria): angry, fight, quarrel, rage, raging, resist, wrath.

riri: fierce, furious.

ririki: neap tide.

riringi: pour.

ri(ri)ngi-hia: pour out, spill.

riiriri: quarrel with one another, wrangle.

riro: taken away, carried off; gone, departed; got, obtained.

riroriro: grey warbler (*Gerygone igata*).

rite: alike, equal; ready; fulfilled, settled; like, resemble.

ritenga: custom, habit, likeness, manner, pattern, practice, resemblance.

riu: bilge, hold of ship; valley.
riiwai: potato.
riwha: chink, cleft, scar; chipped.
riiwhi: relieve, replace, substitute for. **Kai-riiwhi:** reliever, replacement, successor.
roa: durable, length, long, slow, tall.
roanga: continuation, extent.
rohe-a: border of land, boundary.
rohi: loaf (of bread).
rooia: lawyer.
roimata: tear (of weeping).
rooku: log.
roma: current.
roonaki: glide.
rooni(hi): launch (type of vessel).
rongo: fame, famous, gospel, make peace, peace, savour, taste, tidings.
rongoaa: drug, medication, medicine; cure.
rongo-hia, (rangona): feel, sense, hear, obey, smell, taste v.
roopere: strawberry.
ropi: rope.
roopuu: band (musical), company, party group.
roore: lord (in titles).
rore: noose.
rore-a: snare, trap.
ro(o)ri: road.
rori: distorted; foolish; sea-slug.
roria: Jew's harp.

rori(rori): silly; staggering.
roro: brains, marrow, porch.
roroi: grate.
roromi: squeeze.
roto: inland, among, contents, inside, interior, lake.
rouihi: rose (flower).
rourou: basket (small), for cooked food.
ruu: earthquake, shake, vibrate.
rua: two; pit, hole, chasm, burrow, nest (if in a burrow).
ruaki-na: vomit, retch.
ruhi: enfeebled.
Ruuhia: Russia.
rui-a: scatter.
ruku-hia: dive.
ruuma: room.
rumaki-na: duck (someone).
ruumaatiki: rheumatism.
ruunaa: reduce, pare down; close a bag with a draw-string.
runa: dock (*Rumex flexuosus*).
ruunanga: council.
runga: above, over, top; south. **Te Runga-rawa:** God.
rupe: lintel of a doorway = **koorupe.**
ruupeke: assembled, gathered together.
rure-a: wrangle.
rurerure: shake.
rurerure-a: brandish.
ruuri-tia: survey (land); ruler (measure). **Kai-ruuri:** surveyor.
ruu: earthquake.
ruu(ruu): shake, brandish.

ruru: morepork (*Ninox novaeseelandiae*); shelter, take shelter; keep close together.

ruruku-tia: band, headband; to band.

ru(ru)tu: drip, pour out.

ruutene: lieutenant.

T

Taa, taa: Sir, a term of address to respected males, especially knights, but used familiarly in some areas to address young males.

taa-ia, -ngia: mallet, maul; beat, dash down violently, dump; dash water from a boat, bail; to (make a) net; print, tattoo. **Taa ki te perehi:** print, publish.

ta(a): particle marking dominant possession of a single item (LLM, 14, 14.2).

tae (taaea): arrive, reach; achieve, attain, overcome; be able, possible. **Tae noa ki:** until.

taea: tyre.

taaeo: thicket of kiekie or supplejack.

taaepaepa: dangle. **Te taaepaepatanga o te rangi:** the horizon.

taewa: potato.

tahaa: calabash, gourd.

taha: bank of river, beside, pass by, side.

taahae-tia: steal, rob; fellow, rascal.

tahaki: shore, one side.

tahanga: naked.

taahapa: pass by; be left behind; awry, oblique.

tahataha: bank of river, brink.

tahatai: coast, sea-coast, shore.

tahatika: coast.

taahawahawa-tia: contaminate.

tahe: abortion, menses, miscarriage.

taaheke: cataract, rapid, waterfall.

tahi: one; together with.

tahi(tahi)-a: clear away, sweep.

tahu: spouse.

taahuhu: ridgepole.

taahuna: bar of harbour, river, sandbank, shoal.

tahu-na: kindle a fire, light a fire, cook.

taahunga: oakum.

tahuri: overturned, turn, upset.

taahurihuri: restless.

tai: coast (as opposed to inland); sea, tide. **Tai pari:** high tide. **Tai timu:** ebb tide. **Tai aa:** neap tide. **Tai hauaauru:** west coast. **Tai raawhiti:** east coast. **Tai tokerau:** North Auckland. **Wai tai:** sea water.

taiahoaho: light, not dark.

taiapa: fence, field, paddock.
taiapo-tia: covet.
taiari-tia: smash, smashed.
taiatea: faint-hearted.
taiawa: cold (virus).
taiawhio: round about.
taiepa: fence.
taika: tiger.
taikaha: violent.
taaima: time.
taimaha: heavy, weight.
taimana: diamond.
taainahi: yesterday.
taipara: volley.
taipoo: typhoid fever.
tairanga: elevate, elevated.
taairi: hang, be hanging.
taitaa: snag *n.*
taitama: bachelor, boy, young man, youth.
taitamaahine: young woman.
taitamarikitanga: youth (time), childhood.
Taaite: Thursday.
taitea: sapwood.
taka: fall, tumble; prepare; roam.
takahanga: sole of foot.
takahi-a: tramp, trample, tread. Takahi wahine: violate, rape.
takai-a: bandage, bind, pack, wrap up.
takakau: free, single, unattached.
takakino-tia: destroy, ill-treat, spoil.
takapau: floor mat, floor covering.
takapuu: abdomen.

taakaro-hia: game, play, sport.
takataapui: companion of the same sex, friend.
takatuu: prepare.
takawaenga: mediator.
takawiri: twisted (of timber).
takawiri-tia: twist.
takawhetawheta: writhe.
take-a: cause, ground of quarrel, etc., source, stump, subject, reason, matter under discussion.
takere: keel.
taketake: firm.
taake-tia: stack, haystack; tax. Tari taake: tax department.
takihaere: travel.
taakihi: kidney; taxi.
takihii: taxi.
taki-na: challenge.
takini (o te tou): anal sphincter.
taakiri-tia: jerk, start, sudden movement, twitch.
takitahi: singly.
takitaki: recite.
takiwaa: district, interval, region.
tako: gums, palate.
takoki: sprained.
taakoru: fold, hanging in folds.
takoto: desolate, disorderly, empty, vacant.
takotoranga: position, womb.
takoto-ria: lie down.
taaku: my (LLM, 14.3).
taku: my (LLM, 14.3).
takupu: gannet.
takuru: thud.
Takurua: Sirius.
takurua: winter.

taakurukuru: thump.

taakuta: doctor.

takutai: coast, sea-coast, shore.

tamaahine: daughter.

tamaahu: first-fruits.

tamaiti: boy, child, son.
Tamaiti atawhai, tamaiti whaangai: foster-child.

tamariki: children, offspring.

tamarikitanga: childhood.

tama-roto: inner man.

taamaru-tia: cloudy.

tame: boar, male of animals.

taamuimui-a: throng, crowd around.

tamumutia: hum.

taamure: snapper.

taamutumutu: intermittent.

taana: his, hers (LLM, 14.3).

tana: ton; his, hers (LLM, 14.3).

taanakuru: spanner.

taanapu-tia: trump (cards); rear up (of a horse).

taane: father, husband, male, man.

taanumi-tia: fold.

taangari: dungarees.

taangata: men, people.

tangata: man, person. **Tangata whenua:** host, local person (as opposed to guest), aborigine, native.

tangatanga: loose.

tangi-hia: cry, lament, mourn, scream, sound, wail, weep.

tango-hia: take, appropriate, grasp, receive; take off (clothes); subtract.

taangorongoro: blistered, loose.

tangotango: handle, use.

tao: lance, spear *n.*

taokete: brother-in-law, sister-in-law.

tao-na: cook *v.*

taaone: town.

ta(a)onga: goods, merchandise, possessions, property, riches, treasure, wealth; polite term for sex organs.

taapaa: chapped.

tapa: margin, rim.

tapa-ia: call name, name *v.*

taapae-a: place one on another, stack, lay; confess (sins).

tapahi-a: chop, cut, hack.

taapaapaa-tia: pulverise.

taapapa-tia: lie face down, lie prone; a kumara plot.

taapara: double.

tapatahi: single.

tapatapa-ia: bespeak.

taapatu-tia: thatch.

taapau: floor mat.

tapawhaa: square, four-sided.

tapeha: skin.

taaperu: pout.

tapi-a: mend, patch.

taapiri-tia: join, supplement.

taapoa: abscess.

taapokopoko: boggy.

taapoorena: tarpaulin.

tapou: bowed down, dejected, downcast.

taapu: tub.

tapu: under ritual restriction, holy, sacred; prohibited.

tapuhi-tia: carry in the arms, nurse.

taapui-a: appropriate, bespeak, reserve; a mark placed to indicate ownership.

taapuke-tia: bury, cover up.

taapuni-a: mend (of a net).

taputapu: appliances, goods, merchandise, possessions, property.

tapuwae: footprint.

taara: dollar.

tara: peak, point, spine of fish or sea-urchins, etc; tern (*Sterna striata*); female pudenda.

taarai-a: chip, chop, dub out, fashion.

taraipiunara: tribunal.

taraiwa-tia: drive a vehicle.

taraka: truck.

tarakihana: tractor.

tarakitaa: tractor.

taraamoa: bush lawyer (*Rubus* spp.).

taramu: drum.

tarapii: fine (of thread).

tarapu: stirrup, strap.

Tararaa: Jugoslav, Dalmatian.

taratara: prickly, rough; spike.

tarau: pants, trousers.

tarautete: trousers.

tarawaahi: side or bank of river.

taare: doll.

tare: gasp; hang, be hanging.

taareparepa: flap in wind.

tarepoono: telephone.

taretare: ragged.

tarete: thread *n.*

taarewa: hang, be hanging, dangle.

tari: office, study.

taaria: (*See* **tatari**).

taariana: boar, stallion.

taringa: ear; fungus; inattentive.

tarioi: dawdle.

taro: (*Colocasia esculentum*).

taroma: flaccid.

taarona-tia: strangle.

taaruke: impatient.

tarutaru: grass, weed *n.*

taruwhiti: cold (virus).

taataa: shin.

tataa (taaia): bailer, bail; dash, throw down violently, dump.

tata: near, close.

taatahi: coast, sea-coast.

taatai-a: genealogy, lineage; arrange, set in order; adorn.

taataa-kau: unfruitful.

tatakii: viscid.

taa(taa)mi-a: press down upon, suppress, oppress.

tatangi: clatter, jingle, rattle.

tataa-ngia: break in pieces.

taatarahake: bristling.

taatarakihi: cicada.

taataraamoa: bush-lawyer (*Rubus* spp.), bramble.

tatari (taaria): expect, wait.

taatari-tia: sieve, strain, wring.

tatau: door.

tatau-ria, (tauria): count, calculate, figure.

taa(taa)whi-a: hold back (e.g., on a rope); suppress feelings, emotion.

Tatimana: Dutch, Dutchman.

taatou: us, we (including you) (LLM, 9.3).

tatuu: reach the bottom, arrive, be settled.

taatua: belt, girdle.

tatutatu: unsteady.

tau: settle, perch, land, arrive; string, cord; bark (of dog); a kind of song; sweetheart, lover; year, season; suitable.

taaua: us, we (you and I) (LLM, 9.3).

taua: army.

tauapo-hia: hug.

tauaarai-tia: barricade, obstacle.

tauawhi: hug.

tauhoou: novice, stranger; wax-eye (*Zosterops lateralis*).

tauihu: figure-head.

tauira: model, copy, pattern, example; pupil, scholar, disciple.

tauiwi: foreigner.

taumaha: heavy, weight.

taumanu: thwart of a boat.

taumau-tia: betroth.

taunaha-tia: bespeak.

taunu: jeer, mock, revile, taunt.

taunga-tia: accustomed, familiarised.

taupare-a: obstruct.

taupatupatu: beat one another.

taupoki-na: cover, covered, lid; turn upside down.

taupuru: overcast.

taura: rope.

tauranga: anchorage, landing place, mooring.

taurapa: sternpost.

taurekareka: slave.

tauria: (*See* **tatau-ria**).

taurima: fosterchild.

tautau: cluster.

tauteka: brace, prop; carry on a pole.

tautohe(tohe)-tia: contend, quarrel, dispute.

tautoohito: experienced.

tautoko-na: prop, support.

tauwehe-a: separate, remove, divide.

tau(w)era: towel.

tauwhare(whare): overhang.

tauwhaatoo(too): pull one against another.

tawa: a tree (*Beilschmiedia tawa*).

taawaahi: opposite side, other side (of river, sea).

taawai: trot of horse.

taawai-a: sneer, taunt, tease.

tawatawa: mackerel (*Pneumatophorus australasicus*).

taawekaweka: encumbrance.

Taawera: morning star.

taawera: towel.

taaweru: garment, rag.

taaweewee: sound depth of water.

taawiri: tremble, shake; cowardice.

taawhai: imitate; beech (*Nothofagus* spp.).

taw(h)ai: beech (*Nothofagus* spp.).

taawhao: brushwood, scrub; refuse, rubbish.

taawhaowhao: driftwood.

taawharau-tia: shelter.

taawhenua: land breeze.

tawhero: a tree (*Weinmannia sylvicola*).

taawheta: writhe, toss about.

tawhetawhe: old garment.

taawhiri-tia: beckon, whirl.

tawhitawhi: hang back, delay, hesitation.

taawhiti: noose, snare, trap.

tawhiti: distant, distance, far away.

tawhito: old.

taawhiu-a: muster.

tee: break wind, fart; make sharp, explosive or cracking sound; negative marker.

tea: white; clear.

teatea: pale, apprehensive, afraid.

tehe: glans of penis; circumcised penis.

teehea?: which?

teihana: station.

teina, (*pl.* **teeina**)**:** younger sibling of the same sex (hence brother, sister); junior relative.

teitei: height, high, lofty, tall.

teka: dart; falsehood, tell lie.

tekau: ten.

teke: female pudenda, cunt.

teketiwhi: detective.

tekihana, tekiona: section.

tekoteko: carved figure.

teemara: thimble.

teeme: dame.

teme: female pudenda, cunt.

temepara: temple.

teenaa: that (near you) (LLM, 3.2). **Teenaa koe/koorua/ koutou:** good-day to you.

teenei: this (LLM, 3.2).

teeneti: tent.

teenehi: tennis.

teenihi: tennis.

teno: notch.

teepara: stable; staple; table.

tepetepe: clot; jellyfish; tap-dance.

teepu: table; the chair-person.

teputi: deputy.

teeraa: that (yonder) (LLM, 3.2).

teera: tail of animal.

tera: saddle, saddlecloth.

terapu: stirrup.

tere: afloat, float, drift, adrift; glide, sail; quick, rapid, swift, fast, speed; shoal (of fish).

tereeina: train (railway).

tero: anus. **Tero puta:** piles.

terotero: a dish made from intestines; slate.

teetahi: a, an, another, certain, particular (LLM, 43.21).

tetee: gnash.

tetepe: clot.

teetere: trumpet.

tee(w)hea: which?

tii: tea; cabbage-tree (*Cordyline* spp.). **Tii-kaauka, tii-koouka:** (*Cordyline australis*). **Tii-ngahere:** (*C. banksii*).

tia: deer.

tiaho: shine, shining.

tia-ina: stick in, peg; steer.

tiaka: jug.

tiakerete: chocolate.

tiaki: jack (cards); check (bank).

tiaki-na: guard, keep, nurse, protect.

tiamana: chairman.

Tiamana: Germany, German.

tia(a)mu: jam.

tianara: general (officer).

Tiapanii: Japanese.

tiare: scent.

tiaati: charge (with an offence).

tiati: judge *n*.

tieipii: justice of the peace.

tiieke: saddleback (*Philesturnus carunculatus*).

tiemi: see-saw.

tihe: sneeze.

tihehu: disarranged, scattered (as of papers).

Tiihema: December.

tiiheru: bailer.

tiihi: cheese.

tihi: peak, summit.

tiihore: rip.

tiihore-a: flay, skin, pare, strip.

tikaa: cigar.

tika: accurate, appropriate, correct, direct, straight, just, lawful, proper, right, upright.

tikanga: correct procedure, custom, manner, way, method, plan, practice; meaning, significance, reason; authority, control, rule.

tiikaokao: fowl, hen.

tiikaro-tia: scoop out, gouge.

tiikera: kettle.

tiiketi: ticket.

tiketike: height, high, lofty.

tiki, (tiikina). Tiki atu:, go and fetch. **Tiki mai:** come and get.

tiki: carved figure, image. **Heitiki:** human image, generally in greenstone, worn from the neck.

tiikiti: ticket.

tikitiki: topknot.

tiikoko-a: shovel.

tikotiko: diarrhoea.

tiima: team.

tima: steamer.

tiimata: dart *n*.

tiimata-ria, -ngia: begin, start.

tiimatanga: beginning.

timera: chimney.

timo: beak, bill.

timotimo: peck.

timu: ebb, low (of tide).

tina: fast, fixed, lunch.

tinana: body, trunk of tree.

tinei-a: quench fire.

tiineinei: sit on heels.

tiini: chain; gin; change; jeans.

tini: many, multitude, numerous, plentiful; abound; tin.

tinihanga-tia: deceive, dishonest, fraud, jest.

tino: best, exact, very.

tio: oyster.

tioka: chalk.

tiokareti: chocolate.

tiioro: shrill, tingle.

tiotio: prickly.

tiipaki(paki): crack lice or fleas with fingernails.

tiipaata: teapot.

tipi: skim along surface. **Tipi haere:** call in at various places when on a journey.

tipitipi: push-hoe.

tipu: (Eastern dialect form of **tupu** q.v.).

tipuaki: crown of head, top of head.

tiipuna: *pl.* of **tipuna** q.v.

tipuna: ancestor, grandfather, grandmother (Eastern dialect form of **tupuna**).

tira: company, file, row, fin, mast.

tiiraha: lie on back.

tiirairaka: fantail.

tirara: scattered, in disarray, wide apart (of legs); low pitched (of roof).

tirari: scattered, in disarray.

tiiraumoko: bastard.

tiriki-teihana: trig station.

tiringi: string.

tiriti: street; treaty.

tiriwaa-tia: space, interval; to separate, place at intervals.

tiiroa: steering oar.

tiro-hanga: view.

tirohia: (*See* **titiro**).

tirotiro: gaze, peep.

tiitaha: look sideways, sideways; vary; slope, slant, tilt.

tiitaka: unsteady.

tiitakataka: turn over and over.

tiitii: mutton-bird; squeak.

titi: teat, tit, nipple.

titi-a: fasten, penetrate; peg, pin.

tiitipi: glide.

titiro, (tirohia): behold, examine, look, observe, stare.

tito: falsehood, lie; tell a story, sing a song.

tiitongi: nibble; manure.

tiitore-a: tear (rip).

tiuka: duke.

tiuti: duty.

tiiwaha: shout.

tiiwara-hia: cleave, open (as mussels, etc.).

tiwee: scream.

tiiwii: television.

tiwi: dividend.

tiwha: spot.

tiiwhana: curved.

tiwhikete: certificate.

too: your (singular) (LLM, 15.4); stove.

to(o): particle marking subordinate possession of a single item (LLM, 14.1).

too-ia: drag, haul, pull; set (of a heavenly body).

too-iti: little toe.

too-kia: plant in the ground.

toa: bold, brave, courage; warrior; victorious; male of animals; shop, store; door.

tooanga-waka: portage.

toe: remain, be left over.

toenga: balance, remainder, scrap.

tohatoha: distribute.

tohe (toohea): persevere, strive, endeavour.

tohetohe: contentious; uvula.

toohi-tia: toast, propose a toast.

138

tohoraa: whale.

tohu-ngia: point out, direct; sign, signal, symbol, symptom; cherish, spare.

tohunga: skilled person, artisan, expert; priest, wizard.

tohutohu: signs, portents, directions.

toimaha: heavy, weight.

toitoi: fish for eels with a bob; trot (of horse).

toka: rock.

tookari-tia: notch.

toke: worm.

tookena: sock, stocking.

toki: axe, hatchet.

tokomauri: hiccough.

tokopuhake: belch.

tokotoko-na: pole, staff, walking-stick; walk with a stick.

tooku: my (LLM, 14.2).

toma: burial place, cemetery.

toomairangi: dew.

tomo-kia: enter, go in.

tomokanga: entrance, opening.

toomuri: hang back; be late, last.

toona: her, his (LLM, 14.2).

toonapi: turnip.

toone: stone (weight); whetstone.

tono-a: ask for favour, apply for, command, demand, order, send; application, request.

tonu: particle denoting continuity, permanence or exactness (LLM, 22.2, 51).

tonga: south.

tongako: fester.

toongaa-mimi: bladder.

tongi: dot, speck, spot.

tongitongi: speckled.

topa: fly, soar, swoop.

tope-a: cut, chop down, fell.

tore: female pudenda, cunt.

toorea: oyster-catcher (*Haematopus* spp.), pied stilt (*Himantopus leucocephalus*).

toremi: disappear, disappeared, drowned.

torengi: set (of sun).

toretore: inflamed (of eyes).

tori: cat.

toro: blaze, reconnoitre, visit.

toroa: albatross (*Diomedea epomophora*); drawer.

toro-ihi: insolent.

toromi: drowned, be.

toroona: throne.

toro-na: (*See* **totoro**).

toronaihi: sickle.

toropuku: sneak.

toorori: tobacco.

torotoro: run, runner, scout, shoot.

torouka: raw.

toru: third, thirteen, thirty, three.

torutoru: few.

toota: saucer.

tote: salt.

tootika: correct, straight, direct; right.

tootiti: sausage.

totitoti: limp *v.*

tootoo: tow *v.*

toto: bleed, blood.

totohe (toohea): argue, contend.

totohu: sink.

totoka: congeal.

totoro (toorona): reach out, stretch out, extend.

tou: anus.

tou-a: dip; plant *v.*

tuu: manner, kind, sort; wounded.

tuu-ria: stand, stop.

tua: behind a solid object, beyond a solid object, other side.

tuaahine: *pl.* of **tuahine** q.v.

tuahine: sister (man speaking), girl cousin.

tuuaahu: ritual place, altar.

tuuahu-tia: make a mound of earth, mound up into hillocks.

tua-ina: fell, chop down.

tuaina: string.

tuaiwa: ninth.

tuaakana: *pl.* of **tuakana** q.v.

tuakana: older sibling or cousin of the same sex as speaker.

tuaki-na: disembowel.

tuanui: roof, ceiling.

tuangi: cockle (*Chione stutchburyi*).

tuaono: sixth.

tuapae: horizon.

tuapeka: dissimulate.

tuuaapora: first-fruits.

tuaraa: back.

tuararo. Iwi tuararo: backbone.

tuari: dispense, distribute. **Kai-tuari:** steward, waiter.

tuarima: fifth.

tuarua: second, twice.

tuatahi: first.

tuatoru: third.

tuawaru: eighth.

tuawhenua: mainland.

tuawhitu: seventh.

tuuheihei: dishevelled.

tuhi-a: point out.

tuhituhi-a: draw, write, delineate.

tuuhua: obsidian.

tuiau: flea.

tuinga: seam.

tui(tui)-a: sew, thread, fasten together by sewing, lace up.

tuke: angle.

tukemata: eyebrow.

tuketuke-a: nudge; elbow.

tuki: beater, hammer; beat, pound, ram, strike; butt, gore.

tuukinotanga: injury, harm.

tuukino-tia: ill-treat, injure, be injured, maltreat.

tukipuu: general (not specific).

tuki(tuki): beat, pound, ram, strike; mallet, pestle.

tuku-a: free, set free, let down, allow, let go, release, permit, send.

tukupuu: general (not specific)

tuku-roa: backstay.

tukutuku: cobweb, web.

tukutuku-a: slacken.

tuumanako-hia, -tia: hope, expect.

tuumau: cook *n.*

tumera: chimney.

tuumomo: kind, sort, variety.

tumu: stump.

tumuaki: crown of head, top of head.

tuna: eel.

Tunihia: Tunisia.

tunu(tunu)-a: bake, broil, parch, roast, toast, heat, grill.

tuunga: site.

tunga: grub. **(Niho) tunga:** toothache.

tungaane: brother or cousin (female speaking).

tungou: nod.

tuungoungou: chrysalis.

tuuohu: bow, stoop.

tuupaa: unfruitful.

tuupaapaku: corpse.

tuupara: double-barrelled musket.

tuupare: chaplet, garland.

tuupari: cliff, precipice.

tuuparipari: precipitous; steep.

tuupato: careful, caution, cautious, suspicious, suspicion, wary.

tupehau-kia: clumsy, do clumsily.

tupeka: tobacco.

tupeke-tia: leap, jump; gallop.

tupere: pout.

tuuperepere: boisterous.

tuperu: pout.

tuupono: chance upon, befall, happen.

tuuporo: log.

tuupoupou: porpoise.

tupu-ria: grow, sprout; growing shoot of a plant or tuber; real, genuine.

tupua: goblin.

tupuaki: head, top of.

tuupuhi: emaciated, thin, lean; gale, storm.

tuupuna: *pl.* of **tupuna** q.v.

tupuna: ancestor, grandfather, grandmother.

tuuranga: position, standing place, situation.

tuurapa: to spring, move suddenly.

ture: law.

tuurehu: goblin, fairy, mythical being in human form.

Tuurei: Tuesday.

tuureiti: late.

turi: knee; deaf, obstinate, disobedient.

turituri!: hush!, what a noise!, shut up!

turori: stagger.

tuuroro: invalid.

tuuru: chair, seat, stool.

turuawe-poo: midnight.

tuuruhi: tourist.

turuki: follow on, supplement, grow anew (as feathers after a moult), suckers of a plant.

tuururu: crouch.

turuturu: drip, leak.

tuutae: dung, faeces, excrement, shit.

tuutai: scout, spy.

tuutaki-na: come together, meet; close (of a door).

tuutara: gossip.

tute-a: shove.

tuutei: scout, spy.

tutetute: jostle.

tutuu: insubordinate, obstinate, perverse, refractory; mischievous.

tutu: a shrub (*Coriaria arborea*).

tuutuuaa: person of low birth, commoner; ungentlemanly, uncouth, common.

tutuki: complete, be completed, finished; reach the end, or limit.

tuuturi: kneel.

tuuturu: certain, sure, confirmed, constant, permanent.

tuuwai: emaciated, lean.

tuuwatawata: fortification.

tuwha-ia: distribute.

tuwha-ina: spit.

tuuwhenua: a disease mentioned in song and tradition and likened to leprosy.

tuwhera: open, gaping.

U

uu: fixed, firm, fast; female breast. **Mata-uu:** nipple. **Wai-uu:** milk.

uu-ngia: arrive at a place, land (as a vessel).

ua: back of the neck, nape.

ua-ina: rain, shower. **Ua whatu:** hail.

uaua: vein, sinew, ligament; difficult, hard, strenuous.

ue: scull.

ueue: agitate.

uha: female animal.

uhi: (*See* **u(w)hi**).

uho: core.

ui-a: ask question, enquire, inquire.

uira: lightning.

uiui-a: catechise.

uku: clay.

uku-ia: wipe.

uma: bosom, breast, chest.

umere-tia: shout.

umu: oven.

unahi: scale of fish.

uniana: union.

unu-hia: draw out, pull out, withdraw; take off clothes.

unu-mia: drink (Eastern dialects).

uunga: landing place.

unga-a: send.

upoko: head.

upokohue: porpoise.

upoko-roro: grayling (*Prototroctes oxyrhynchus*).

ure: penis.

uri: descendant, offspring, progeny.

uru: hair; head.

uru-a: enter, participate; grove.

urunga: pillow.

urungi-tia: helm, steer; rudder.

urupaa: cemetery, tomb, burial ground.

ururua: overgrown.

urutaa: epidemic, pestilence.
urutapu: untouched.
urutira: dorsal fin.
uta: ashore, inland, interior of a country, shore.
uta-ina: load.
utanga: cargo.
uutonga-tia: calloused.

utu-hia: avenge, revenge, pay, price, wages, salary, fee; fill a vessel with liquid.
uwha: female animal, sow.
uwhi: yam.
u(w)hi-a: cover, covered; table-cloth.
uwhiuwhi-a: sprinkle.

W

Note: Words beginning with WH are listed separately.

waa: period of time, time, season; interval, space, region.
waea: wire.
waea-tia: telegram, telephone.
waenga: middle.
waenganui: amidst, among, between, centre, middle, midnight.
waere-a: clear off vegetation, remove obstacles.
waerehe: radio, wireless.
waerenga: clearing in bush.
waereti: violet.
waeroa: gnat, mosquito.
waewae: foot, leg, stilts.
waha-a: carry on the back.
waha: mouth.
wahaika: a type of club.
waahanga: division.
wahanga: load carried on back.
wahapuu: entrance, mouth of river.

waharoa: gateway.
waahi: place, locality.
waahi-a: part, piece, portion.
waahia: (*See* **waawaahi**).
wahie: firewood.
waahina: virgin.
waahine: women.
wahine: female human, lady, wife, woman.
waho: eject, out, outer, outside.
wai: water, liquid, juice. **Wai maaori:** fresh water. **Wai tai:** salt-water, sea-water. **Wai-uu:** milk. **Wai-ariki:** mineral spring.
wai?: who?, whom? (LLM, 16.6).
waia: familiarised, acquainted with, practised; skill, expertise.
wai(ata): (*See* **waiata-tia**).
waiata-tia: sing, song; traditional chant as opposed to **waiata-a-ringa**, modern action song; psalm, as

opposed to **hiimene**, hymn. The shortened form **wai** refers to the song or chant that concludes a formal speech.

wai-hakihaki: mange.

waihape: tack (of a sailing ship).

waiho-tia: leave, put, place, lay, remain.

waikeri: ditch, drain.

waikura: rust.

waimarie: luck, lucky, fortunate.

waimeha-tia: insipid; dilute.

waaina: wine.

waina: vine.

waingoohia: easy.

waipuke-tia: flood.

waipuna: spring (of water).

wairaakau: manure; dye from sap of trees.

wairanu: gravy.

wairangi: foolish, over-excited, crazy.

wairua: soul, spirit.

waitau: mouldy.

waitutu: dark (in colour).

waka: boat, canoe, conveyance, vehicle; spirit medium.

wakarere: aeroplane, plane, aircraft.

waakena: waggon.

waaki, waakihi: wax.

waaku: my = **aaku**.

wani-a: comb, graze, scrape.

waanihi: varnish.

waapi: wasp.

waapu: wasp, wharf.

waarati: warrant.

ware: plebeian, non-chiefly, ignorant; exudation, secretion, saliva, sap.

ware-a: distract, distracted, occupied, unaware.

warehenga: kingfish (*Seriola grandis*).

wareware: forgotten, unmindful.

wareware-tia (ki): forget.

waariu: value. **Hekenga waariu:** depreciation.

waro: charcoal, coal, embers.

waru: eight.

waru-hia: peel, scrape.

waata-kirihi: water-cress.

waataropa: wardrobe.

waatea: free, unoccupied, vacant; available.

wati: watch *n.*

wawaa: paling.

wawae-a: separate, sever.

waawaahi-a (waahia): split, cleave, divide; wrench (tool).

wawao (waona): defend; mediate between or separate antagonists.

wawata-tia: desire.

wawe: too soon, prematurely.

wehe(wehe)-a: divide, separate; separation, schism.

wehi: fear, fright, dread, timid.

weka: wood-hen (*Gallirallus* spp.).

weekete: waistcoat.

Wenerei: Wednesday.

wene(wene): young shoots of gourd plants.

wepu-a: flog, whip.

weera: whale.

wera: heat, hot, burnt.

werawera: warm; perspiration, sweat.

wereweti: velvet.

weri: centipede.

weriweri: abominable, disagreeable, loathsome, offensive, vile.

wero-hia: pierce, prick, stab, sting.

wete (wetekia, wetekina): (*See* **wewete**).

Weeteriana: Wesleyan.

weeti: wedge; weigh, weight.

wetiweti: abominable, loathsome; relish.

weto: extinguished.

weu: fibre.

wewete (wetekia, wetekina):
loosen, disentangle, unravel, untie.

wiihara: whistle.

wihiki: whisky.

wiki: week; fuse, wick.

wikitooria: victory.

wini: glass, window; win.

winika: vinegar.

winiwini: shudder.

wiira: wheel.

wira: will, last testament.

wiri(wiri): auger, drill, gimlet; bore, drill; quake, shiver, tremble.

wiriwiri: vibrate.

wiiti: wheat.

Wiiwii: France, French.

wii(wii): rushes (*Juncus* spp.).

wuuru: wool.

wuruhi: wolf.

WH

whaa: four.

whaaea: mother, aunt.

whai (whaaia): follow, pursue.

whai: stingray; cat's-cradle, string-games.

whaiaaipo: sweetheart.

whaikoorero-tia: orate, oration.

whaina-tia: fine (legal).

whaainga: goal, that which one pursues or aims at.

whaaiti: compact, narrow.

whaitiri: thunder.

whaiuru: file (implement).

whaiwhaiaa: witchcraft, black magic.

whaiwhai-a: chase, hunt.

whaaka: fork.

whakaea(ea)-tia: take breath, respire; requite, pay for.

whakaeke-a: assault, invade, attack.

whakaemi-a: gather together, assemble.

whakaene-tia: make smooth; present the backside as a mark of contempt.

whakaero-tia: dwindle, diminish; putrefy.

whakaae-tia: accede, acknowledge, agree to, approve, assent, consent.

whakaeto: evaporate.

whakahaere-a: conduct a case, business, direct, manage, conduct, control.
Kai-whakahaere: conductor (legal).

whakahanumi-tia: mix.

whakaharihari: make merry.

whakahau-a: command, exhort, order.

whakahauhau: encourage.

whakahauora: refresh, revive.

whakahaawe-a: despise.

whakaheke-a: let down, lower; decrease. **Whakaheke tupu:** diminish in importance.

whakahemo-a: complete, consume entirely, be finished.

whakahee-ngia: blame, condemn, contradict, criticise, object.

whakahere: offering.

whakahiihii: arrogant, conceited, haughty, proud; pride, vanity.

whakahinuhinu: glossy.

whakahinga-ia: demolish, overthrow.

whakahipahipa: irregular, of different lengths or heights.

whakahirahira: extol; magnificent, astonishing, wonderful.

whakahoa-tia: associate with, be friendly with.

whakahoohaa: nuisance, bother.

whakahoki-a: answer, reply, return, turn back.

whakahoonore-tia: honour v.

whakahori-a: disbelieve.

whakahoro-a: demolish, cause to crumble, dismantle.

whakaho(ro)horo-tia: accelerate, hasten.

whakahotuhotu: pant, gasp.

whakahouhou: detest, feel disgust; loathsome.

whakaahua-tia: form, fashion; portray, portrait, photograph.

whakahua-tia: pronounce, recite.

whakaahuru: cherish.

whakaihi-a: betroth, set apart, dedicate.

whakainu-mia: give drink, cause to drink.

whakaipo(ipo)-tia: court, woo; cherish.

whakairi-a: hang something up, suspend, suspended.

whakairo-hia: carve, figure, sculpt.

whakaiti-a: lessen, decrease.

whakakaha: enable, strengthen.

whakakaahore-tia: abolish, annul, deny, forbid, object, refuse.

whakakai: cylindrical greenstone pendant, suitable for a teething child to bite on.

whakaakakahu-ria: dress, clothe.

whakakakara-tia: to scent, perfume.

whakakake-a: arrogant, boast, haughty, proud.

whakakaaniwha-tia: notch, so as to form a barb, fashion a barb.

whakakapi-a: successor, substitute; fill up a space.

whakakeke: persist in resisting; sulk.

whakakeko: aim (as a gun).

whakakiikii: persuade.

whaka(ki)kii-a: fill, cram full.

whakakikii-tia: tighten; grasp.

whakakikiwa: keep the eyes firmly closed.

whakakino-tia: abuse, abusive; disapprove, dislike, hate.

whakakite-a: disclose, display, reveal, show.

whakakoi-a: sharpen.

whakaako-na: instruct, teach, educate.

whakakopa(kopa)-ia: clasp, clutch; fold up, wrap up.

whakakoopee-tia: squeeze.

whakakoopeke-tia: cool, make cold.

whakakorakora-tia: scatter.

whakakore-tia: deny; cause not to be, annihilate; abolish, nullify.

whakakooroiroi: hinder.

whakakorokoro-tia: slacken off, loosen.

whakakoromeke-tia: coil up, loop up.

whakakoorua-tia: hollow out, excavate.

whakakotahi: unite, make one.

whakamaa: abashed, ashamed, shame, shy.

whakamahana-tia: warm, heat up.

whakamahara-tia: remind, remember.

whakamahau: verandah, porch.

whakamahi-a: set to work.

whakamahu: heal.

whakamaimoa: fondle.

whakamaakuukuu-tia: moisten.

whakamamae-tia: hurt, inflict pain, torment; feel pain, be in labour.

whakamana-a: acknowledge authority, enable.

whakamanawa-tia: encourage.

whakamaanu-tia: launch a boat.

whakamaaoa-tia: to cook.

whakamaaori-tia: interpret, translate.

whakamaarama-tia: explain.

whakamaarietanga: consolation.

whakamaarie-tia: propitiate, soothe, appease.

whakamaaroo: stretch, extend; wire strainer.

whakamaroke-tia: to dry.

whakamarumaru: shade, shelter.

whakamataku-ria: fright, frighten, frightened, scare, terrify.

whakamaataotao-ria: to cool, make cold.

whakamatara: unravel.

whakamaatau-ria: attempt, prove, try, test.

whakamaatautau-ria: tempt; examination.

whakamau-a: fasten.

whakamauru: subside.

whakamiiharo-tia: amazing, astonishing, wonderful; admire, wonder at.

whakamihi-a: thank; commend, compliment, praise.

whakamine-a: assemble, congregate, gather together (of people).

whakaminenga: assemblage, assembly, crowd.

whakamoe-a: put to sleep; give in marriage, marry off.

whakamoomori: desperate, desperation; commit suicide.

whakamootii: destroy, destroyed, exterminate.

whakamua: ahead, forwards. **Haere whakamua:** advance.

whakamuri-a: backwards. **Hoki whakamuri:** go back, retreat.

whakamutu-a: conclude, finish, cause to cease, stop.

whakanaa: satisfy.

whakananawe: dawdle, hold back; fasten, make fast to.

whakananu-a: adulterate, mix; confuse.

whakanoa-tia: remove tapu, render common; desecrate.

whakanoho-ia: establish, put in place.

whakanui-a: enlarge, magnify; exalt, ennoble.

whakangaa: take breath; refresh.

whakangahau-tia: entertain, entertainment.

whakaangaanga: undecided.

whakangaoko: tickle; amuse.

whakangaro-mia: conceal, hide; exterminate, annihilate.

whakangau-a: hunt with dogs; strike at, strike against.

whakangaawari-tia: soften.

whakaangeingei: peep.

whakaangi: fly kite.

whakangoikore: enfeeble, enfeebled.

whakaoho-kia, -tia: arouse, awaken, startle.

whakaongaonga: excite, goad.

whakaora-ngia, -tia: cure, heal; deliver, save.

whakaoti-a: conclude, complete, finish.

whakapae-a, -ngia: accuse; suspect; lay across; besiege.

whakapai-a, -ngia: approve, bless, praise, thank; put in order, fix, make good, improve.

whakapaipai-tia: adorn, embellish, tidy, prettify; ornamental, beautiful.

whakapakari: mature (of people).

whakapaa-kia: touch; obstruct, close up.

whakapaakanga: last-born child.

whakapakoko-tia: mummify, dry, embalm; idol, image, statue.

whakapaparanga: layer.

whakapapa-tia: genealogy, lineage; lay one on another.

whakaparahako-tia: disdain, refuse, reject.

whakapaataritari: excite, incite.

whakapati(pati): coax, flatter, wheedle, beg, cadge.

whakapau-ngia: consume, exhaust, finish up, use up.

whakapee: crush.

whakapiata-tia: polish.

whakapiko-a: bend, bent.

whakapiri: fasten to, stick to; remain close to.

whakapooheehee-tia: confuse.

whakapokorua-tia: hollow out.

whakapono-ngia: belief, believe; faith, trust; truth.

whakaponotanga: proof.

whakapoto-a, -hia: abbreviate, abridge, shorten.

whakapuu: stack.

whakapuaki-na: disclose, reveal; utter.

whakapuare-tia: open.

whakapuumau-tia: establish, make permanent.

whakapuru-a: to pad; saddle-cloth.

whakaputa: boast; release, let out. **Whakaputa kee:** change, alter.

whakaara-hia, -tia: arouse, awaken, wake up; raise.

whakaranu-a: adulterate; mix with.

whakarangatira-tia: ennoble, enhance status.

whakarapa-ngia: stick, be stuck, adhere.

whakararikena: rascal, larrikin.

whakararu-a: confuse, confused, disturb.

whakararuraru: hinder.

whakarato: serve out (e.g., food).

whakarawa-tia: fasten with a latch or bolt.

whakarawe-a: close, fasten up (e.g., a kit).

whakarere, (whakareerea): abandon, change, forsake, cast off, leave, reject.

whakarere: suddenly.

whakarewa-ia: launch (as a boat).

whakarewa-ina, -tia: melt (as grease).

whakaari-a: display, expose, show.

whakarihariha: abominable, disagreeable, loathsome, vile; loathe; disgust.

whakaariki. Ko te whakaariki!: warning cry on seeing an approaching war-party.

whakariro-ia: pervert, alter.

whakarite-a: adjust, appoint, arrange, compare, correspond to, match, liken to; decide, ordain; comparison, simile, parable.

whakaaroaro: ponder, consider carefully.

whakaroa-tia: lengthen, extend; linger, loiter.

whakaaro-hia: consider, suppose, meditate, think, thought, opinion; offering, present.

whakaaro-kore: careless, thoughtless.

whakaaro-nui: wise, wisdom.

whakarongo-hia: attend, listen, obey.

whakaropiropi: a hand-game.

whakaruaki: emetic.

whakaata: reflection, look at a reflection, reflect.

whakataa: breath, take breath.

whakataetae-ngia: race, contest, competition.

whakatahataha: turn from side to side.

whakatahe-a: miscarriage, aborted foetus; to abort; drain off (as water).

whakatahuri-ngia: convert.

whakatairanga-tia: elevate.

whakataairi: hang something up.

whakataakaro-tia: amuse.

whakataakotokoto-ria: arrange.

whakatakoto-ria: lay down; plan something.

whakataamaramara: swagger.

whakaatamira-tia: lay out, of a corpse.

whakatangatanga: free, set free.

whakatangitangi-hia: to play a musical instrument.

whakatapu-a, -ria: sanctify, consecrate, hallow, cherish.

whakatara-a: tease, defy.

whakataritari: incite, provoke.

whakatata-ngia: approach.

whakatatae: compete.

whakatau-a: examine; decide; visit; command; decision.

whakataukii: proverb, saying.

whakaatea: clear away.

whakateka: disbelieve.

whakatenetene: annoy, provoke.

whakatete: molest, annoy, pick a quarrel with.

whakatika-ia: arise, rise up; straighten, correct.

whakatiimata-ngia: initiate.

whakatina-ia: oppress.

whakatiitaha: tilt.

whakatoohenehene: disarrange.

whakatoi: annoy, tease, give cheek.

whakatoo-kia: to plant.

whakatoomuri: loiter.

whakatopa: hover, soar.

whakatuma: defy.

whakatuupato-ria: warn.

whakatuupehupehu: bluster.

whakatupuranga: generation.

whakatupu-ria: to grow, rear.

whakatuu-ria: erect, instigate; boast, propound.

whakaatu-ria: point out, show, draw attention to, reveal, disclose, inform, show, tell, testify.

whakatuturi: unyielding.

whakatutuki: complete, finish.

whakatuwhera-tia: to open.

whakauaua: exert oneself, strive, toil.

whakauu-ngia: fasten, fix, make fast.

whakauru-a: insert.

whakaurunga-tia: lean against.

whakautu-a: answer.

whakawahi-a: anoint.

whakawai-a: beguile.

whakawaa-kia: to judge, adjudicate.

whakaware-a: beguile.

whakaware-a: distract, distracted.

whakawaatea-tia: make available, clear.

whakawaawaa-tia: wrangle; recriminate.

whakawehi-a: scare, frighten, terrify, threaten.

whakawairangi: crazy, foolish.

whakawerawera: to warm.

whakawiri-a: wring.

whakawhaanau-tia: bear, give birth.

whakawheruu-tia: encumber, encumbered, hinder.

whakawheetai: thank.

whakawhirinaki-tia: lean against, support.

whakawhiti-a: to cross.

whakawhitinga: a ford.

whakawhitiwhiti: alternate.

whakawhiu-a: oppress, afflict.

whakawhiwhi-a: wind round, fasten.

whaaki-na: admit, own up, confess, disclose, reveal, tell.

whakiwhaki: pick, gather (as fruit), tear off.

whana-a: recoil, spring; kick.

whaanako-tia: rob, steal, thieve; thief.

whanariki: sulphur.

whanatu: go.

whaanau: be born, bear (a child); (extended) family.

whanaunga: kin, relation.

whaanautanga: birth.

whanowhanoaa: vex, vexed, annoyed.

whaanui: broad, extensive, wide.

whanga (ki): wait, lie in wait.

whanga: estuary, open bay (arch).

whaangai-a: feed, rear child, foster, adopt. **Tamaiti whaangai:** adopted child.

whangawhanga: troublesome.

whango: hoarse.

whao: nail, chisel.

whaona: passive form of **whawhao** q.v.

whaowhia: passive form of **whawhao** q.v.

whara: hit, hurt, injured, struck, wounded.

whaarahi: extensive.

whaarangi: leaf of a book, page of book; a tree (*Brachyglottis repanda*).

wharangi: a tree (*Melicope ternata*).

wharara: lean against, stoop.

wharau: shed, temporary shelter.

whare: house, building, residence, dwelling. **Whare-herehere:** prison, jail.

Whare-karakia: church.
Wharekura: school. **Whare ngaro:** a family with no issue, an extinct line.
Wharenui: a meeting-house.
Wharepuni: a meeting-house.
wharewhare: overhanging, of a wave or a bank.
whaariki-tia: carpet, floor mat, to cover a floor with mats or carpet.
wharo: cough, clear the throat; that which is expectorated, phlegm.
whaarua: valley.
whata-a: stage, shelf, place for storing; shelve, put up on.
whati: fracture, fractured, broken, snapped off; interrupted (of speech).
whaatiia: (*See* **whawhati**).
whatianga: angle, elbow, portion doubled over or broken off.
whatitiri: thunder.
whatitoka: doorway.
whaatoro: reach out.
whatu: stone of fruit, kernel of nut, hailstone; pupil of eye, eye; core of a boil.
whatu-a: weave using the technique known as finger-weaving.
whaatui: lace or tie together.
whaturama: swelling such as a rupture, hernia or scrofulous swelling.
whawhai-tia: fight, oppose, quarrel, resist; battle, war, affray.

whawhaki: pluck, pick (as fruit).
whaawhaa-ria: feel, touch, handle, grope for.
whawhao (whaowhia, whaona): to fill (as a bag); stuff in.
whawhati (whatiia): fracture, snap off, break cleanly.
(w)hea?: where?
wheeangaanga: undecided.
wheekau: bowels, entrails, guts, intestines.
wheke: octopus. **Nguu-wheke:** cuttlefish, squid.
wheketere: factory.
wheekii: a tree-fern (*Dicksonia squarrosa*).
whekuwheku: splashed with water, wet.
whenua: country, land, ground; afterbirth.
whengu: snort.
wheo: buzz.
wheoro: rumble, reverberate, make a crashing sound (as of thunder). **Wheoro te taringa:** said of buzzing of mosquito in one's ear.
wherahia, wheratia: (*See* **whewhera**).
wheeraa-tia: like that, treated like that.
whererei: protrude (e.g., of eyes, anus).
wheriko: glisten.
whero: red (including reddish-brown and orange); anus.
wherowhero: reddish.
wheruu: encumbered, oppressed by encumbrances.

whetau: dodge.

whetee: be forced out (e.g., of core of a boil, of eyes in war-dance); stare wildly.

wheti: rounded, pot-bellied.

whetuu: star.

whetuurangi-tia: appear above horizon (as a star, the moon).

wheua: bone.

wheewhee: boil or abscess.

whewhenge: withered, shrivelled.

(w)hia?: how many?

whika: arithmetic; figure.

whiinau: a tree (*Elaeocarpus dentatus*).

whio: whistle; blue duck (*Hymenolaimus malacorhynchos*).

whioi: groundlark (*Anthus novaeseelandiae*).

whiiore: tail of animal but not of a fish.

whira: fiddle, violin.

whiri-a: plait (as a rope), twist.

whiriwhiri-a: choice, choose, pick, select, discuss.

whiro: willow.

whiiroki: thin, lean.

whiti: physically fit; verse, stanza.

whiti-a, -ngia: cross over (as a river, bridge); shine, shining (as sun).

whiitiki-ria, -tia: belt, girdle; gird, put on a belt; tie round (as a head-band).

whitu: seven.

whiu: surfeited.

whiu-a: cast, throw, fling; flog, toss; lash, punish, whip, thresh.

whiwhi: acquire, gain, obtain; possess, be fortunate in possessing; be fastened, entangled.

whoroa: floor.

whoounu: telephone.

whuruu: influenza.

whurupeeke: fullback.